Easy English!

Series Editor

Adrian Wallwork
English for Academics SAS
Pisa, Italy

Easy English is a series of books intended for students and teachers of English as a foreign language.
More information about this series at http://www.springer.com/series/15586

Adrian Wallwork

Jokes

Have a Laugh and Improve Your English

Springer

Adrian Wallwork
English for Academics SAS
Pisa, Italy

ISSN 2522-8617   ISSN 2522-8625   (electronic)
Easy English!
ISBN 978-3-319-67246-5   ISBN 978-3-319-67247-2   (eBook)
https://doi.org/10.1007/978-3-319-67247-2

Library of Congress Control Number: 2017963152

© Springer International Publishing AG 2018
This work is subject to copyright. All rights are reserved by the Publisher, whether the whole or part of the material is concerned, specifically the rights of translation, reprinting, reuse of illustrations, recitation, broadcasting, reproduction on microfilms or in any other physical way, and transmission or information storage and retrieval, electronic adaptation, computer software, or by similar or dissimilar methodology now known or hereafter developed.
The use of general descriptive names, registered names, trademarks, service marks, etc. in this publication does not imply, even in the absence of a specific statement, that such names are exempt from the relevant protective laws and regulations and therefore free for general use.
The publisher, the authors and the editors are safe to assume that the advice and information in this book are believed to be true and accurate at the date of publication. Neither the publisher nor the authors or the editors give a warranty, express or implied, with respect to the material contained herein or for any errors or omissions that may have been made. The publisher remains neutral with regard to jurisdictional claims in published maps and institutional affiliations.

Printed on acid-free paper

This Springer imprint is published by Springer Nature
The registered company is Springer International Publishing AG
The registered company address is: Gewerbestrasse 11, 6330 Cham, Switzerland

Student's Introduction

What Is *Easy English*?

Easy English is a series of books to help you learn and revise your English with minimal effort. You can improve your English by

- reading texts in English that you might well normally read in your own language e.g. jokes (this book), personality tests, lateral thinking games, wordsearches.
- doing short exercises to improve specific areas grammar and vocabulary, i.e. the areas that tend to lead to the most mistakes - the aim is just to focus on what you really need rather than overwhelming you with a mass of rules, many of which may have no practical daily value.

What Level of English Do I Need in Order to Benefit from This Book?

If your level is intermediate and above, then you should be able to understand the majority of the jokes, apart perhaps from those that are based purely on word play.

One massive benefit of jokes is that they are generally short and also contain a lot of dialogue. The sentences are also simple in structure. Even if you don't understand the joke the first time you read it, re-reading it only involves another 30 seconds of your time.

How Will This Book Help Me Improve My English?

The aim of this series is to enable you to do something you would have done in your own language and can have fun doing in English. The added benefit is that in reading the jokes in this book, you will learn a lot of new vocabulary and revise your knowledge of grammar.

Jokes are great for learning vocabulary, expressions and grammar.

Jokes are also designed to be retold. If you learn a joke by heart and tell it to other people, then by doing so you will also learn the grammar involved in a specific context which should help you to remember the rules.

Because jokes are short, you can read them quickly. So this is the kind of book that you can pick up and put down easily. You can set yourself any easy task such as to read two jokes a day. Most other kinds of reading exercise require much more time and dedication on the part of the reader.

How Will I Know Whether I Have Understood the Joke or Not?

The first test is whether you smiled or laughed!

In any case, the jokes contain a related exercise designed to reveal whether you have understood the joke or not. Typical exercises include:

- A joke is presented to you but with the paragraphs mixed up. Your task is to put them in the correct order. This obviously entails you understanding the structure of the joke.
- The joke has a choice of three punch lines. If you select the correct one, this should be an indicator that you have understood the joke.
- The joke has the verbs in the infinitive form (or a choice of two forms). Your task is to choose the correct form/tense.
- Several two-line jokes are presented together. You have to match the first line and the second line.
- A joke is presented with some key words missing. You have to insert the right word in the right place.

Obviously in some cases you will not 'get' (i.e. understand) the joke. Bear in mind that this might not be a language problem, but simply that you cannot see the humor in the joke (because the joke for you is not actually funny). In any case, if you don't understand the joke, this is a great opportunity for you to ask a native speaker to explain it to you.

How Difficult to Understand Are the Jokes in This Book?

The chapters are not in any order of difficulty.

Student's Introduction

The jokes that appear in this book are authentic. This means that they have not been adapted to suit a non-native learner. However the jokes that have been selected do not generally contain much slang, and the 'bad' language has been reduced. The overall idea was to give you an opportunity to experience jokes in the same way as a native speaker might experience them.

Jokes by nature require a good knowledge of the language. They also contain some unusual words. However this does not mean that you will not be able to 'get' (i.e. understand) the jokes.

How Funny Are the Jokes?

This is an impossible question to answer.

The main purpose of this book was not simply to make you laugh, but to improve your English. However, I hope you like my selection of jokes.

My criteria for choosing the jokes was that they had to make me smile and/or contain some useful vocabulary, phrase, or example of grammar usage. Humor is totally subjective. Some jokes may make you laugh out loud (I hope!), others may amuse you a little less, others (a minority I hope) you may think are not funny at all.

What Should I Do if I Don't Understand Some of the Words in the Joke?

Below each joke is a list of words (glossary). This glossary is shaded in grey and contains words that you might be unfamiliar with plus their definitions. Note: These definitions are for the word as it is used in the particular context of the joke.

If the word you don't know is not in the glossary, then try using context.reverso.net to see the word used in context and the various translations into your own language.

Alternatively do a Google search. In the search box, simply type in the word followed by 'definition'. This will automatically generate a definition.

You can also hear the pronunciation of the word by clicking on the sound icon - both for Google and context.reverso.

How Should I Use the Glossaries at the End of Each Chapter?

These glossaries list alphabetically the words in the mini-glossaries (shaded in grey throughout each chapter). You can use them to:
- check whether you remember the meanings of the words of phrases. To do this, simply cover the right-hand column
- use the white space between the words and their definitions in order to write down the translation of the word/phrase

Note: The glossaries only contain the definition of the word/phrase as used within the context of the joke.

How Does a Joke Work?

A joke typically takes the form a story, generally with dialog. A joke is generally structured in three stages as follows:
1) a setting - the context, scene and characters of the joke are established. This setting may be well already familiar to the listener, as many jokes on a similar topic follow an identical or very similar structure. This stage of the joke will also probably indicate who, if anyone, is going to be the 'butt' of the joke. The 'butt' means the target, the person/s who we are going to laugh at. Typical butts of jokes are lawyers (and other professions), drunks, stupid people, and unfortunately women (though I have reversed the trend by focusing mainly on jokes where men, rather than women, are the target).
2) false expectation/interpretation - the joke leads you to expect a certain outcome.
3) punch line - this is the final line/sentence of the joke, which gives a conflicting meaning to the expectation/interpretation of stage 2.

How Do People Typically Introduce a Joke?

If you want to recount one of the jokes in this book to another person, you could begin, as a native-speaker would begin, by saying one of the following:

That reminds me of a joke I know/a joke I heard. ...
Have you heard the joke about ...?
Do you want to hear a good joke ...?
So, there's an engineer, a computer programmer and an elephant ....

What Comments Do People Typically Make After Hearing a Joke?

If they don't understand the joke, they might say: "I don't get it"

So you need to prepare an explanation of the joke for the eventuality that someone doesn't understand it.

If they think the joke is unsuitable, they might say: "Oh, that's bad".

In this case you may think you need to justify why you thought the joke was acceptable/appropriate.

If they like the joke, they might say: "That was a great joke, where did you get it?"

In this case 'get' means 'find'.

If I Tell a Joke Do I Need to Use the Exact Same Wording as the Original Joke?

No. But you do need to stick to the same structure. And be careful that the punch line is as close to the original as possible. In fact, even if you tell the joke badly (e.g. you forget a couple of words, you hesitate, or you start again), the joke can still be funny providing that you get the punch line correct.

What Kind of Jokes Are Included in this Book?

The book contains no racist jokes and I have tried to avoid jokes that might be considered not politically correct. However, given the male dominated world we live in, women are far more frequently the butt of jokes than men. I have tried to compensate for this by including several feminist jokes.

In any case, I apologize if by chance you do find any jokes in this book that you consider to be unsuitable in some way.

What Tenses Tend to Be Used in Jokes?

Jokes tend to told in two tenses: the present simple and the past simple. As you know, the PRESENT SIMPLE is usually used in English to talk about a regular event:

> I walk to university on foot.
> She plays tennis every day.
> We live on the third floor.

In the context of jokes, the present simple is known as the historical present. It is used to make the joke/story come alive. It's as if we are participating in the situation, or at least observing it first hand. Here is an example:

> A man walks into a bar and orders a beer. After a few minutes he says to the bartender, "Hey, if I show you the most amazing thing you've ever seen, will you give me another beer on the house?" "We'll see," said the bartender, "I've had a lot of strange people come in here, and I've seen some pretty amazing things in my day." So the man pulls out a hamster and a tiny piano from his briefcase, and puts them on the bar. Then the hamster begins to play Chopin. "Not bad," said the bartender, "but I'll need to see more." "Okay, hold on," says the man as he pulls out a frog from his briefcase. Suddenly the frog starts singing "My Way." A patron nearby jumps up from his table and says, "That's amazing! I'll give you $1,000 right now for that frog!" "Sold!" says the man, who exchanges the frog for the cash. The bartender then says to the man, "You know, it's none of my business, but I think you just gave away a real fortune in that frog." "Not really," says the man, " the hamster is also a ventriloquist."

The historic present is the tense that drives the joke forward and recounts the main actions.

However, within the joke itself, other tenses can be used. The above joke also contains examples of the present perfect and the future using *will*:

> *The most amazing thing you've ever seen.* (present perfect: previous experience from the past leading up to the present moment)
> *I've had a lot of strange people come in here, and I've seen some pretty amazing things in my day.* (present perfect: previous experience not specifically related to a single point of time in the past)
> *Will you give me another beer on the house?* (*will* used as a request)
> *I'll need to see more.* (*will* to indicate a decision made now)
> *I'll give you $1,000 right now* (*will* to indicate a decision made now, an intention)

Student's Introduction

The other tense used to recount the main actions of a joke is the past simple, sometimes in combination with the past continuous which indicates something that was already taking place when a second action intervened. Below is an example:

> A boy with a monkey on his shoulder was walking down the road when he passed a policeman who said, "Now, now young lad, I think you had better take that monkey the zoo." The next day, the boy was walking down the road with the monkey on his shoulder again, when he passed the same policeman. The policeman said, "Hey there, I thought I told you to take that monkey to the zoo!" The boy answered, "I did! Today I'm taking him to the cinema."

Note that in the above joke, the short actions are expressed using the past simple: *passed*, *said*, *answered*. The long actions, in this case *walking*, are expressed by the past continuous.

What Are the Other Books in this Series? Which One Should I Read Next?

Currently there are six books in the series.

> Jokes - *have a laugh and improve your English*
> Test your personality - *have fun and learn useful phrases*
> Wordsearches - *widen your vocabulary in English*
> Word games, riddles and logic tests - *tax your brain and boost your English*
> Top 50 grammar mistakes in English - *how to avoid them*
> Top 50 vocabulary mistakes in English - *how to avoid them*

These books are designed to be dipped into rather than being read from the first page to the last. 'Dipped into' means that you can pick up the book and read any page you like, and for as long as you like.

You are likely to have more fun with the books if you read two or three at the same time. So rather than spending the next month reading 200 jokes or learning/revising 100 words, you might find it more fun and stimulating to read a few jokes one day, and do a few wordsearches or word games the next day.

Teacher's Introduction

Why Use Jokes?

Jokes are very motivating for students. They are short (generally) and memorable. And because they are designed to be retold, your students can practice telling them and at the same time learn, for example, some grammar usage (see *What tenses are used in jokes?* in the Student's Introduction).

You can do lots of other joke-related activities:

- Students can translate jokes from their own language into English and discuss the difficulties of doing so (puns, culture etc.)
- Students can try and explain the humor to each other
- As a class, you can analyze how jokes are typically structured (see next subsection)
- You can analyze the use of vocabulary e.g. often synonyms are used in jokes, particularly for the main characters (*this guy ... so the man ... and then the bloke*), in order for the teller to create variety and not to have to keep repeating the same word
- You can teach the language associated with jokes (*butt, quip, punch line* etc.) and the expressions typically used to talk about or react to a joke, e.g. *I didn't get it. D'you get it? I didn't find it very funny. That's so funny!*

How Do Jokes Work? How Are they Structured?

Jokes are designed to play with the listener's expectations. If I ask you:

> What do zebras have that no other animals have?

Your first thought is likely to be stripes, given that no other animals have stripes. But actually the answer is 'baby zebras'. It is the unexpected answer that makes you laugh.

Again, if I ask you:

> How do you get an elephant into a matchbox?

This will set your brain thinking about the massive size of an elephant and the impossibility of it ever being able to get inside a matchbox. And you start trying to think of some 'logical' answer, even though the situation is clearly absurd. The answer is in fact: Take out all the matches first.

Some jokes come in pairs or in a series. The first joke gets you to think in one way, and then the second reveals that you were headed in totally the wrong direction:

> How do you get two whales in a Mini?
> One in the front, one in the back.
> How do you get two ants in the same Mini?
> You can't. It's full of whales.
> How do you get four whales in a Mini?
> Two in the front, two in the back.
> How do you know when a whale is visiting your house?
> There's a Mini outside with four whales in it.

Below is a snippet of dialog from the movie *Four Weddings and a Funeral*. The dialog begins:

> A: So, John, how's that, how's that gorgeous girlfriend of yours??
> B: She's no longer my girlfriend.

When you hear "She's no longer my girlfriend" you imagine that they have broken up, or for some reason they are no longer together. In a real situation your inclination might be to offer some form of condolence, which is what John's friend does:

> A: Oh dear. Still, I wouldn't get too gloomy about it. Rumor has it she never stopped bonking old Toby de Lisle just in case you didn't work out.
> B: She's now my wife!?
> A: Excellent! Excellent! Congratulations!

So all the time, the joke is taking you in one direction before suddenly hitting you with a totally unexpected outcome.

[The analysis of the joke owes much to Francisco Yus's analysis of the same joke in his paper *A relevance-theoretic classification of jokes*. Yes, jokes are also widely studied in academia!]

You can get students to analyze the jokes you give them in a similar way to the Four Weddings joke analysis.

How Can I Exploit a Joke in the Classroom?

Read this joke and think how you could exploit it in the classroom. Imagine that you have pre-taught any key vocabulary (e.g. *furniture importer, four-poster bed*).

> On the last night of his first buying trip to Paris, a young furniture importer from America met an attractive French girl in the hotel elevator. She spoke no English, however, and neither of them could understand a word the other was saying.
> So the resourceful merchant devised a means of communication for the occasion. Taking out a pencil and a notebook, he drew a sketch of a taxi. The girl nodded approvingly, and off they went for ride in the Bois de Boulogne.
> A little later, he drew a picture of a table laden with food and wine bottles, and when she nodded her assent, they headed for a sumptuous meal at Maxim's. After dinner, she was delighted with a sketch he made of a dancing couple, so they danced the evening away at a popular Left Bank night club.
> Finally, the girl picked up the pencil and, with a knowing glance at her clever escort, she proceeded to make a crude drawing of what was clearly intended to be a four-poster bed. He stared at his charming companion in amazement.
> When he took her home, while he was kissing her goodnight on her doorstep, during the long ride back to his hotel, and even on his flight back the following afternoon, he still couldn't figure out how she had known he was in the furniture business.

Below are some ideas. You could:

- Add two more punch lines and give students three alternatives to choose from.
- Scramble the five paragraphs and put them into the correct order.
- Put once sentence in the wrong position. Students then have to find the sentence and relocate it to its correct position.
- Delete words (or phrases or complete sentences), put them in a box, and get students to insert them in the correct places.
- Put students in pairs and get them to explain the meaning of the joke to each other - they may have interpreted it in different ways.
- Ask them specific vocabulary questions. For example: Which adjective+noun combinations are used to refer to the man? [Answer: young furniture importer, resourceful merchant, clever escort] And which to the woman? [Answer: attractive French girl, charming companion]. You then discuss why synonyms are used in jokes.
- Put some of the verbs in brackets for students to put in the correct tense.
- Ask students to learn the joke (or another joke) at home and recount it in the next lesson.

How Can I Practice Grammar Using Jokes?

You can create a tense usage exercise in one of the following ways:
- A man and his wife *traveled/were traveling* down the highway when they *saw/were seeing* the lights. [Students choose the correct tense].
- A man and his wife *travel* down the highway when they *see* the lights. [Students convert the infinitive form into the correct form].

You can focus on just distinguishing between two tenses, or between multiple tenses. For example the following joke contains six different forms of the verb (highlighted in italics).

A prisoner in jail receives a letter from his wife:
"Dear husband, I *have decided* to plant some lettuce in the back garden. When is the best time to plant them?"
The prisoner, *knowing* that the prison guards *read* all mail, replies in a letter:
"Dear wife, whatever you do, do not touch the back garden. That is where I *hid* all the money."
A week or so later, he receives another letter from his wife.
"Dear husband, you *wouldn't believe* what happened. Some men came with shovels to the house and *dug* up the back garden." The prisoner writes back:
"Dear wife, now is the best time to plant the lettuce."

The following joke, like many jokes, contains a lot of dialog. Students could put what the characters say into reported speech. You can limit the number of sentences by indicating them italics.

Sherlock Holmes and Dr Watson go on a camping trip. After a good dinner and a bottle of wine, they retire for the night, and go to sleep. Some hours later, Holmes wakes up and nudges his faithful friend.
"*Watson, look up at the sky and tell me what you see.*"
"*I see millions and millions of stars*, Holmes" replies Watson.
"*And what do you deduce from that?*"
Watson ponders for a minute. "Well, astronomically, it tells me that there are millions of galaxies and potentially billions of planets. Astrologically, I observe that Saturn is in Leo. Horologically, I deduce that the time is approximately a quarter past three. Meteorologically, I suspect that we will have a beautiful day tomorrow. Theologically, I can see that God is all powerful, and that we are a small and insignificant part of the universe."
"But what does it tell you, Holmes?"
Holmes is silent for a moment.
"*Watson, you idiot!*" he says. "*Someone has stolen our tent!*"

The amount of work you expect from your students will obviously depend on their level. In the next joke, if as part of your exercise you used all the verbs that I have put in italics, it would take quite a lot of time for students to put them into the correct

Teacher's Introduction xvii

tense. First they would need to work out the meaning of the joke, and then have to make some complex decisions regarding the tenses. Also, there would be a lot of repetition as many of the verbs are repeated and require the same tense as they are in the same context. So limit the task.

> George *was going* to bed when his wife *told* him that he*'d left* the light on in the shed. George *opened* the door *to go* turn off the light but saw there were people in the shed in the process of *stealing* things. He immediately *phoned* the police, who *asked*, "*Is* someone in your house?" and George said, "No," and *explained* the situation. Then they *explained* that all patrols *were* busy, and that he *should simply lock* his door and an officer *would be* there when available. George *said*, "Okay," *hung* up, *counted* to 30, and *phoned* the police again. "Hello, I just *called* you a few seconds ago because there *were* people in my shed. Well, you *don't have to* worry about them now because *I've just shot* them all." Then he hung up. Within five minutes three squad cars, an Armed Response unit, and an ambulance *showed* up. Of course, the police *caught* the burglars red-handed. One of the policemen *said* to George, "I *thought* you *said* that *you'd shot* them!" George said, "I *thought* you *said* there *was* nobody available!"

In addition to limiting the number of verbs to be put in the correct tense, another way of making the task easier is to show students two versions of the same joke - the clean version which they read first, the tense correction version which they read second. They can then compare their answers with the clean version:

> A man was going to bed when his wife told him that he'd left the light on in the shed. George opened the door to go turn off the light but saw there were people in the shed in the process of stealing things.
> He immediately phoned the police, who asked, "Is someone in your house?" George said, "No," and explained the situation.
> The police then explained that all patrols were busy, and that he should simply lock his door and an officer would be there when available.
> George said, "Okay," hung up, counted to 30, and phoned the police again:
> "Hello, I just called you a few seconds ago because there were people in my shed. Well, you don't have to worry about them now because I've just shot them all."
> Then he hung up.
> Within five minutes three squad cars, an Armed Response unit, and an ambulance showed up. Of course, the police caught the burglars red-handed.
> One of the policemen said to George, "I thought you said that you'd shot them!"
> George said, "I thought you said there was nobody available!"

The way the joke is laid out may also effect the difficulty of the task - as highlighted by the two versions of the George joke above.

Punch Lines

One exercise that I have used a lot in this book is for students to choose the right punch line. This is a good exercise, because generally speaking if a student has chosen the correct punch line it probably means that they understood the joke.

Choosing the correct punch line is best done in pairs or groups, as this promotes discussion and involves students explaining their interpretation of the joke to each other.

Occasionally students might legitimately be able to argue that their punch line is correct, even though the key suggests otherwise. Below is an example where the first two punch lines would both be possible.

> A man is charged with first-degree murder and is on the stand, being questioned by the prosecution.
> "Did you commit the crime?"
> "No sir, I did not."
> "I remind you that you are under oath. Do you know the penalty for perjury?"
>
> a) "Yes sir, and it's considerably less than the penalty for murder."
> b) "Yes sir, I didn't do it and I'll never do it again."
> c) "Yes sir, and my lawyer explained to me how I couldn't possibly have committed the crime."

Do I Need to Adapt the Language of the Jokes or Will that Lose Their Authenticity?

The same joke often appears in many different formats, so I think it is perfectly legitimate to adapt jokes for use in class. The jokes in this book have only been very slightly modified to remove any potentially obscure, embarrassing or racist vocabulary.

If you are preparing lessons using jokes you've found on the internet, you could even insert vocabulary that students have learned in recent lessons - you just need to be a bit creative!

What Types of Jokes Are Not Included in this Book?

This section outlines the reason why certain types of joke were not included in the book.

Teacher's Introduction   xix

Racist and Anti-Women Jokes

I read thousands and thousands of jokes while compiling this book. Around 75% of the jokes I read were racist or anti-women. For what I hope are obvious reasons I didn't want to include such jokes.

However, you might still consider using such a joke in the class, if your intention was actually to stimulate a discussion on racism. You tell ask your students that the joke in question could potentially be considered racist and get them to discuss:

- Why might this joke be considered racist? Against who?
- What are the possible consequences of telling a racist joke (or a joke against any particular minority)?
- Are there any circumstances when it would be legitimate to tell such a joke?

If your students are not convinced that racist jokes can have serious consequences, then get them to read the text below taken from a sociology text book.

> The devastation of Hiroshima and Nagasaki was made publicly acceptable by the fact that the victims were of an 'oriental race'. It was unthinkable that the Americans or the British would have dropped the Bomb on their white European enemies in Germany. But the Japs were different. Throughout the war, they were treated as a lower form of human life. American newspapers, tabloids and broadsheets alike, routinely referred to the Japanese as 'mad dogs' and 'yellow vermin'. Cartoons usually depicted them as monkeys, but also as insects, reptiles and even bats. In every Hollywood war film, the Japanese where portrayed as sadists and war criminals.
> The US and British forces in the Pacific war put these racial ideas into action. One American veteran described the Japanese - 'small, a strange color' - as the 'perfect enemy: 'Marines did not consider they were killing men. They were wiping out dirty animals.' Since that view dominated Western opinion, Hiroshima was widely celebrated as the wiping out of dirty animals on the grand scale. The success of the US and British authorities in instilling their people with the racial attitudes of the Empire ensured that they could kill two hundred thousand Japanese civilians without worrying about serious protests at home. After all, who cares what happens to mad dogs and vermin?

Wikipedia explains that Irish jokes derive from the historical period when Ireland was under British rule:

> The "Irish joke" originates in the simian portrayal of Irish people in British comic magazines of the mid-late 19th century - depicting the Irish as stupid apes given to agrarian and alcohol-fuelled violence against their benevolent and tolerant British masters. In the context of the 'Laissez Faire' policy of the Great Famine and the following mass displacement of the following three decades, a great many Irish view the Irish joke as, at best, offensive and, at

worst, as similar to "n-word" jokes against blacks, or holocaust jokes targeted at Jews. All these forms of humor have, at their core, the debasement of their subjects to the point of dehumanising them so that malevolent acts against them are less offensive - or even justifiable.

However, this book does contain some 'anti' jokes. There are several anti-men jokes (my aim being to compensate for the huge numbers of anti-women jokes) and anti-lawyer jokes - I believe that both groups are fair game for such jokes, but I realize that this is rather a subjective statement to make!

If you are interested in discussing racism in the classroom, then you might like to read my book on taboo/controversial topics from the *Discussions AZ* series, originally published by CUP, but which I am now updating. The units in question are: *H2: Neighbourly jokes* and *X4: Extreme humor*. For details contact me at: adrian.wallwork@gmail.com

National Stereotypes

Whether a joke is racist of just poking fun at a particular nationality is very subjective. Below are some jokes said by various Europeans by other Europeans. They are taken from an article that appeared in an article from the British newspaper The Guardian. The article was entitled: *'Crude but rarely nasty' The jokes Europeans tell about their neighbours.* You can download the full article here:

https://www.theguardian.com/world/2016/may/08/crude-but-rarely-nasty-the-jokes-europeans-tell-about-their-neighbours

In brackets is the nationality that tells the joke.

> "If you knew how to cook and clean," says a Greek husband to his wife, "I wouldn't need a maid." "If you knew how to make love," replies the wife, "I wouldn't need a Macedonian lover." (Macedonians)
> German footballers are like German food: if they're not imported from Poland they're no good. (Poles)
> How do you tell an extrovert Finn? It's your shoes he's looking at, not his. (Estonians).
> How do all Dutch recipes begin? Borrow six eggs, 200 g of flour, half a liter of milk ... (Belgians)
> In a recent survey, 11 out of 10 Spaniards said they felt superior to the others. (Portuguese).

> The main difference between Austrians and the Germans is that Germans would like to understand Austrians but can't, and Austrians understand Germans but would rather not. (Austrians)
> What does a Czech need to be happy? Not much, as long as everyone else has got less. (Slovaks)
> What's the difference between the Swedes and the Finns? The Swedes have got nice neighbors. (Finns)
> What's the best ever thing to have come to Denmark from Sweden? An empty ferry. (Danes)
> Why do Belgians have pommes frites, while the Arab world has oil? Because the Belgians got to choose first. (Germans)

So why didn't I include such jokes? The above jokes are pretty harmless, but in a classroom you may have different ethnic groups or nationalities, or even people of the same nationality but who come from a different town or region. Such jokes can spark off hostility between students, with some students becoming the butt of jokes by other students. This is clearly not an atmosphere you want to create.

Political Jokes

Any discussion of politics can potentially be dangerous in a classroom, given that your students may have very different ideas both from each other and from you. However, political jokes can be interesting from another point of view.

In David Belios's excellent book on the art of translation, entitled *Is that a fish in your ear?* and published by Penguin Books (2011), he quotes the following joke:

> Stalin and Roosevelt had an argument about whose bodyguards were more loyal and ordered them to jump out of the window on the fifteenth floor. Roosevelt's bodyguard flatly refused to jump, saying, "I'm thinking about the future of my family." Stalin's bodyguard, however, jumped out of the window and fell to his death. Roosevelt was taken aback. "Tell me, why did your man do that?" he asked. Stalin lit his pipe and replied: "He was thinking about the future of his family, too."

Belios notes that the joke is a translation from Russian "and even in Russian it's a translation already, because exactly the same joke has been told over the centuries about other brutal potentates, starting with Peter the Great". You could use this joke as an opportunity to talk about how jokes get updated, recycled and adapted to new situations. For example, in Italy where I live and work, during a recent referendum a whole series of jokes that were invented in the Thatcher era in the UK, were adapted to the current situation in Italy.

Jokes that Have Gone out of Fashion and/or are too Culturally Dependent

If you are as old as me you will remember all those jokes deriding Ladas - a brand of cars produced by a Russian manufacturer and which between the 1960s and 1980s were famous for always breaking down. Here are some examples:

> What do you call a convertible Lada?
> A skip.
> How do you double the value of your Lada?
> Fill it up with petrol.
> Why does a Lada have a heated rear windscreen?
> To keep your hands warm while you're pushing it.

I haven't included such jokes precisely because the historical and cultural references would be lost on students today.

The same historical period also bred a lot of jokes about nuclear war, unilateral disarmament, and hippies. The hippy jokes included this one:

> A hippy goes into a cafe and asks for a piece of cake.
> The assistant replies: "The cake's all gone".
> The hippy retorts: "Crazy, I'll have two pieces".

I still love this joke and it takes us nicely into the next section of jokes to be avoided - those that are a little too surreal or offbeat for most students.

Jokes That Rely Totally on Word Play or Are Overly Surreal

There are many jokes that are not included in this book simply because I think the vast majority of students would have great difficulty understanding them and even if they did understand them might not even find them funny.

One joke type that I didn't include, precisely for the above reasons, is the "What do you call?" series. Here are some examples (not all of which are politically correct!).

> What do you call a man who has been buried for 2,000 years?
> Pete.
> What do you call a man with his legs chopped off at the knees?
> Neil.
> What do you call a woman with a toothpick in her head?
> Olive.

Teacher's Introduction

> What do you call a man who is being electrocuted?
> Buzz
> What do you call a man who sits at your front door?
> Matt.
> What do you call a man who has his head stuck under your car?
> Jack.

Some of these "What do you call?" jokes run in a mini series.

> What do you call a man with a shovel in his head?
> Doug.
> What do you call a man with out a shovel in his head?
> Douglas [doug-less].
> What do you call a man with a wooden head?
> Edward.
> What do you call a man with three wooden heads?
> Edward Woodward.
> What do you call a man with four wooden heads?
> I don't know, but Edward Woodward would.

The above jokes also spawned a series of animal-related jokes, some of which are quite surreal. Again your students may find them unfathomable.

> What do you call a sheep with no legs?
> A cloud.
> What do you call a dog with no legs?
> It doesn't matter what you call him - he still won't come.
> What do you call a polar bear in the jungle?
> Lost.
> What do you call two elephants on a bicycle?
> Optimistic.
> What do you call a deer with no eyes?
> No idea
> What do you call a deer with no eyes and no legs?
> Still no idea

Unfathomability, or rather a lack of it, is key to English language teaching. No task that you give you students should make them end up feeling stupid or inadequate. If you are doing a lesson on jokes, then one of the key aims should be for students to get the joke. You certainly don't want to perversely demonstrate that your own intelligence/sense of humor (both on a personal and national level) is superior to that of your students.

Your aim, I believe, is to make your students feel good about their knowledge of English, feel good about themselves, and feel good about you the teacher.

What Other Similar Books Might I Find Useful?

If you teach children and young teenagers, they you might be interested in my book of word games called *Mindtwisters* (published by Scholastic).

Various games and discussion exercises for older teenagers and adults can be found in *Discussions AZ* (two volumes: intermediate and advanced, published by Cambridge University Press).

There is also a series of discussion, warm up exercises, fillers etc published by *SEFL* (sefl.co.uk).

Ideas for Other Books for this Series

If you have any ideas for other books that could be part of the *Easy English* series then please email me.

The Author

Since 1984 Adrian Wallwork has been teaching English as a foreign language - from General English to Business English to Scientific English. Although he lives and works in Pisa (Italy), through his university work he has taught students of all nationalities. Adrian is the author of over 30 textbooks for Springer Science+Business Media, Cambridge University Press, Oxford University Press, the BBC, and many other publishers. He can be contacted at: adrian.wallwork@gmail.com

Acknowledgements

Huge thanks to Anna Southern who removed over thirty pages of 'inappropriate' jokes from this book. Her female sensitivity combined with many years doing jobs requiring a high level of diplomacy, probably saved my bacon, my reputation, and my publisher's reputation!

Thanks also to all those people who upload jokes onto the web, from where the vast majority of these jokes were sourced.

Contents

1 Animals, Bars, and Food 1
2 Doctors. 15
3 Drunks, Idiots and Husbands 29
4 Knock Knock. 41
5 Professions. 57
6 Men and Women. 77
7 School 99
8 Light Bulbs, Waiters, What's the Difference? 117

Index. 135

Chapter 1
Animals, Bars, and Food

In joke 1 the key words below have been removed. Insert them into the correct position.

advertisement
applicant
dictation
interviewer
language
multinational
spreadsheets

1

A dog applied for a job as a high-powered secretary with a _____ company. The _____ stated that the successful _____ must have good keyboard skills, a command of shorthand, and be able to speak a second language. The _____ sat the dog at the computer and watched in wonderment as the animal successfully carried out the most complex functions, including _____ and e-mail. Then he gave the dog _____ and was impressed by the hound's ability to write a hundred and twenty words a minute in immaculate shorthand. "Well," he said at the end of the interview, "It looks as if the job's yours. There's just one thing. What about the second _____ ?" To which the dog replied: "Meow!"

[applied for - replied to a job advertisement; high-powered - a secretary to someone high in the company hierarchy; shorthand - a way of writing using symbols instead of words, once frequently used by secretaries and journalists; wonderment - a mix of surprise and joy; hound - synonym for 'dog'; meow - sound made by a cat]

Many English jokes are set in a bar. A conversation typically takes place between the barman and some person who comes into the bar. A variation of this joke, is that it is an animal that comes into the bar rather than a human being. The animal can talk.

In jokes 2 and 3 below, the joke depends on a double meaning connected to the sound / pronunciation of certain words (<u>underlined</u> in the jokes below). See if you can understand the joke, and then check with the key.

2

A guy walks into a bar with a giraffe and says, "A beer for me, and one for the giraffe, please." So they proceed to drink. Then: "…a shot for me and one for the giraffe, too." And they keep drinking all evening. Finally the giraffe passes out on the floor of the bar. The guy pays for the drinks and gets up to leave. The bartender shouts out, "Hey! You're not going to leave that <u>lying</u> on the floor, are you?" The guy replies "That's not a <u>lion</u>… it's a giraffe."

[shot - small glass of strong alcohol; pass out - faint, go to sleep]

3

A polar bear walks into a bar. The bartender asks what he'll have. The bear says "guess I'll have a ……………. ……………. ……………. beer."

The bartender asks "Why the big <u>pause</u>?"

The polar bear replies. "I don't know, I was born with them."

In jokes 4-11, each joke is followed by three possible punch lines (a, b and c). Choose the punch line which best matches the joke.

4

A magician is working on a small cruise ship. He's been doing his shows every night for a year or two now. The audiences appreciate him, and they change often enough for him not to worry too much about new tricks. However, there's this parrot who sits in the back row and watches him night after night, year after year.

Finally, the parrot figures out how the tricks work and starts giving it away for the audience.

For example, when the magician makes a bouquet of flowers disappear, the parrot squawks "Behind his back! Behind his back!"

Well, the magician gets really annoyed at this, but he doesn't know what to do.

One day, the ship springs a leak and sinks. The magician manages to swim to a plank of wood floating by and grabs on. The parrot is sitting on the other end of the plank. They just stare at each other and drift. They drift for 3 days and still don't speak.

On the morning of the fourth day, the parrot looks over at the magician and says:

a) "OK, I give up. Where did you hide the ship?"
b) "So, what kind of magic trick have got to get us out of this situation?"
c) "Where exactly are we going?"

[figures out - understands; squawk - sound made by parrots; springs a leak - has a hole in its side that lets the seawater in; plank - flat piece of wood; floating - on the surface of the sea; grabs on - holds; drift - to move with the motion of the sea]

5

A father and his small son were standing in front of the tiger's cage at the zoo. The father was explaining how ferocious and strong tigers are, and the boy was taking it all in with a serious expression.

"Dad," the boy said finally, "if the tiger got out of his cage and ate you up …"

"Yes, son?" the father said expectantly. And the boy finished:

a) "What bus should I take home?"
b) "What will mummy say?"
c) "How will I ever manage without you?"

[take in - absorb information]

6

A butcher notices a dog in his shop. He shoos the dog away. But later the dog comes back again. So the butcher goes over to the dog, and notices that the dog has a note in his mouth.

He takes the note, and it reads "Can I have 12 sausages and a leg of lamb, please. The money is in the dog's mouth." The butcher looks inside and, lo and behold, there is a ten pound note there. So he takes the money, and puts the sausages and lamb in a bag, placing it in the dog's mouth.

The butcher is very impressed, and since it's close to closing time, he decides to shut up shop and follow the dog. So off he goes. The dog is walking down the street, when he comes to a level crossing. The dog puts down the bag, jumps up and presses the button. Then he waits patiently, bag in mouth, for the lights to turn. They do, and he walks across the road, with the butcher following him all the way. The dog then comes to a bus stop, and starts looking at the timetable.

The butcher is in awe at this stage. The dog checks out the times, and then sits on one of the seats provided. Along comes a bus. The dog walks around the front, looks at the number, and goes back to his seat. Another bus comes. Again the dog goes and looks at the number, notices it's the right bus, and climbs on. The butcher, by now open-mouthed, follows him onto the bus. The bus travels through the town and out into the suburbs, the dog looking at the scenery. Eventually he gets up, and moves to the front of the bus. He stands on two back paws and pushes the button to stop the bus. Then he gets off, his groceries still in his mouth. Well, dog and butcher are walking along the road, and then the dog turns into a house.

He walks up the path, and drops the groceries on the step. Then he walks back down the path, takes a big run, and throws himself -Whap!- against the door. He goes back down the path, runs up to the door and -Whap!- throws himself against it again. There's no answer at the house, so the dog goes back down the path, jumps up on a narrow wall, and walks along the perimeter of the garden. He gets to the window, and beats his head against it several times, walks back, jumps off, and waits at the door.

The butcher watches as a big guy opens the door, and starts yelling at the dog and hitting it.

The butcher runs up, and stops the guy. "What the hell are you doing? The dog is a genius. He could be on TV, for heaven's sake!", to which the guy responds:

a) "Genius - you've got to be joking this is the second time this week that he's forgotten his key!"
b) "You're right. He once had his own TV show, but he bit the presenter."
c) "Yes, he is in the Guinness Book of Records as the dog with the highest IQ".

[level crossing - place where a road meets a railway track; in awe - very impressed; checks out - consults; paws - dog equivalent of feet; groceries - food that the dog has bought]

7

A guy spots a sign outside a house that reads "Talking Dog for Sale." Intrigued, he walks in.

"So what have you done with your life?" he asks the dog.

"I've led a very full life," says the dog. "I lived in the Alps rescuing avalanche victims. Then I served my country in Iraq. And now I spend my days reading to the residents of a retirement home."

The guy is flabbergasted. He asks the dog's owner, "Why on earth would you want to get rid of an incredible dog like that?"

The owner says:

a) "Because he never stops talking".
b) "Because he's a liar! He never did any of that!"
c) "Because he makes me feel guilty for not having made anything of my own life".

[intrigued - very interested; avalanche victims - people who were killed when stones/snow/mud falls down the side of a mountain; flabbergasted - very surprised]

8

A man walks out on his front porch one day and sees a gorilla in the tree on his front lawn. He telephones the Animal Control Unit, and about an hour later a man shows up with a ladder, a pit bull, and a shotgun.

The Animal Control employee tells the man: "I'm here to get the gorilla out of your tree. I'm going to use this ladder to climb up the tree and shake the branch the gorilla is on to knock him to the ground. The pit bull is trained to go after anything that falls from the tree and bite their balls."

The man says "Okay, I understand what the ladder and the pit bull are for, but what is the shotgun for?"

The animal control employee says:

a) "If anyone comes in the vicinity, shoot in the air - that should scare them away."
b) "The shotgun has a tranquillizer bullet in it. If the gorilla gets violent, shoot it."
c) "Oh, that's for you. In case I fall out of the tree instead of the gorilla, shoot the dog."

[porch - covered space outside front door; lawn - grass in front of a house; shows up - arrives; pit bull - type of violent dog; shake - move quickly; ladder - used for climbing up and down; balls - testicles; scare - frighten]

9

Dracula decides to have a competition to see which of his bats is the best. All the bats take part in this competition. The rules are simple. The bat which sucks more blood than the others is the winner.

The first bat goes and comes back after 10 minutes. Its mouth is full of blood.

Dracula says, "Congratulations, how did you do it?"

The bat says, "Do you see that tower? Behind it there is a house. I went in and sucked the blood of all the family."

Dracula says, "Very good".

The second bat goes and comes back after 5 minutes. Its face is covered in blood. Dracula is shocked, "How did you do that?"

The bat replies, "Do you see that tower? Behind it there is a hotel. I went in and sucked the blood of all the guests."

Dracula says, "Fantastic."

Now, the third bat goes and comes after just 1 minute. All of its body is covered in blood. Dracula doesn't believe his eyes, "How did you do that?"

The bat replies, "Do you see that tower?"

Dracula replies, "Yes."
And the bat says:

a) "Well, I didn't."
b) "Well I can't".
c) "Well I don't".

> [bat - type of animal, like Batman; suck blood - what a vampire does]

10

A man goes on a trip to Europe, leaving his brother at his house to take care of his cat. The man phones home to see how things are.

His brother says, "Your cat's dead."

The traveling brother says "That's a terrible way to tell bad news. I can't believe you'd ruin my vacation like that. I'll show you a better way. You could have said, 'The cat's on the roof and we can't get her down.' Then when I call the next day, you say, 'well, we got her off the roof, using ladders, but it doesn't look good. The cat is not recovering well.' When I call the third day, you say, 'We did our best, the vet tried everything, but the cat passed on.' See how that's a better way to tell me?"

"Yes, yes," the brother says. "You're absolutely right. I'm sorry."

"Okay. So how's everything else?"

a) "Mom's not very well."
b) "Well, Mom's on the roof and we can't get her down."
c) "Mom's dead."

> [ruin - make something go bad; roof - the top of a house; vet - animal doctor; pass on - die]

Joke 11 is followed by two possible explanations (a, b) of what the joke means (i.e. why it is funny). Choose the correct explanation.

11

Two hunters are out in the woods when one of them collapses. He doesn't seem to be breathing and his eyes are glazed. The other man pulls out his phone and calls emergency services.

He gasps to the operator: "My friend is dead! What can I do?"

The operator in a calm, soothing voice replies: "Take it easy. I can help. First, let's make sure he's dead."

There is a silence, then a shot is heard.

Back on the phone, the hunter says, "OK, now what?"

a) The hunter has totally misinterpreted what the operator has instructed him to do. When the operator said 'make sure he's dead' the operated didn't mean for the hunter to kill his friend, but to check whether his friend was still alive.
b) The hunter's ringtone is the sound of a shot being fired.

> [hunter - someone who shoots animals; glazed - opaque]

There is no task for jokes 12, 13, and 14. Simply enjoy! See the key for an explanation if you don't "get" the joke.

12

A gorilla walks into a pub in London, pulls up a stool, and orders a pint of beer. The landlord pours him his beer and says: "That'll be ten pounds". As the gorilla is paying for his pint, the landlord adds: "You know, we don't get many gorillas in here." To which the gorilla replies: "At ten pounds it's hardly surprising".

> [landlord - owner of the pub; pint - a liquid measurement less than a liter; ten pounds - ten euros, ten dollars = very expensive for a beer]

13

Two goldfish are in a tank. One turns to the other and says: "Do you know how to drive this thing?"

> [tank - has two meanings: i) a recipient holding fish ii) an armored vehicle]

14

Little Johnny sat playing in the garden. When his mother came out to collect him, she saw that he was slowly eating a worm. She turned pale.

"No, Johnny! Stop! That's horrible! You can't eat worms!"

Trying to convince him further, "Now the mother worm is looking all over for her nice baby-worm."

"No, she isn't," said Johnny.
"Why not?"
"Because I ate her first!"

The six paragraphs in joke 15 are in the wrong order. Can you put them in the right order?

15

About ten minutes later, he returns and goes to the bar. Again, the man asks for a pint and a pork pie. The barman gladly serves him, and the man drinks his pint, picks up his pork pie, puts it on top of this head and walks out with it balanced on his head.

After five minutes, a second man walks into the pub and asks the barman for a pint and a pork pie. The barman replies, "Sorry, we don't have any pork pies left, will a packet of crisps be OK?". The man says 'Sure, a packet of crisps will be fine.'

A man walks into a pub and asks for a pint and a pork pie. The barman gives him his pint, and a nice fresh pork pie. He drinks his pint, picks up his pork pie, puts it on the top of his head, balances it and walks out.

The man replies "Because there are no pork pies left!"

The second man drinks his pint, then takes the crisps out of the packet and starts balancing them on his head.

Unable to contain his confusion any longer, the barman asks "Excuse me, why are you balancing those crisps on your head?"

Jokes 16, 17 and 18 are all connected with food and restaurants. Match the jokes with the punch lines (a, b, c).

[pint - a liquid measurement less than a liter, pork pie - typical food served in British pubs; crisps - thin slices of fried potatoes typically offered free in pubs]

16

Benny had told all his friends about the delicious steak he'd eaten in a new restaurant the day before. So they all decided to go down there and see if it was really as large and delicious as he said. But much to their disappointment, the waiter brought them the tiniest steak they'd ever seen. Benny called over the waiter and said: "I was in this restaurant yesterday and you served me a really big steak, and now today, when I've organized a party, you serve such a small one." "Yes, sir," replied the waiter. " _____ "

[steak - portion of meat; tiniest - very, very small]

17

A man and a woman were having dinner in a fine restaurant. Their waitress, taking another order at another table, noticed that the man was slowly sliding down his chair and under the table, with the woman acting unconcerned. The waitress watched as the man slid all the way down his chair and out of sight under the table. Still, the woman dining across from him appeared calm and unruffled, apparently unaware that her dining companion had disappeared. After the waitress finished taking the order, she came over to the table and said to the woman, "Pardon me, ma'am, but I think your husband just slid under the table." The woman calmly looked up at her and replied firmly: " _____ "

[slide down - moving down the chair; unconcerned - apparently not worried; unruffled - not worried; slid - past tense of slide]

18

A man was travelling in a foreign country and he was interested in trying out some new food. As he was walking around the town where he had just arrived, he saw a sign saying: *Your wish is our command - we will cook anything you want.* So he decided to go and try out the restaurant. On his way there he tried to think about what he could order. When he got to the restaurant he called the waiter over and said: 'I'd like rhinoceros tongue on toast please.' 'Certainly, sir,' replied the waiter and he went to the kitchen with her order. After a couple of minutes he came back and said: " _____ "

[your wish is our command - we will do whatever you desire; rhinoceros - very large animal]

a) 'I'm very sorry sir but we can't prepare that dish for you - there's no more toast.'
b) "But yesterday you were sitting by the window."
c) "No he didn't. He just walked into the restaurant."

Key to Chapter 1

1

A dog applied for a job as a high-powered secretary with a multinational company. The advertisement stated that the successful applicant must have good keyboard skills, a command of shorthand, and be able to speak a second language. The interviewer sat the dog at the computer and watched in wonderment as the animal successfully carried out the most complex functions, including spreadsheets and e-mail. Then he gave the dog dictation and was impressed by the hound's ability to write a hundred and twenty words a minute in immaculate shorthand. "Well," he said at the end of the interview, "It looks as if the job's yours. There's just one thing. What about the second language?" To which the dog replied: "Meow!"

2

Hey! You're not going to leave that lying on the floor, are you?" The guy replies "That's not a lion… it's a giraffe = 'lying' and 'lion' have a very similar pronunciation

3

pause = paws (i.e. the feet of an animal)

4 a

5 a

6 a

7 b

8 c

9 c

10 b

11 a

12

The landlord is saying that having gorillas in a bar is not very common. The gorilla implies that it is not to do with the strangeness of having a gorilla in a pub, but is due to the high price.

Key to Chapter 1 11

13

'Tank' can mean a recipient for fish but also an armored vehicle.

14

We are expecting to hear why the mother worm is not looking for her baby.

15

A man walks into a pub and asks for a pint and a pork pie. The barman gives him his pint, and a nice fresh pork pie. He drinks his pint, picks up his pork pie, puts it on the top of his head, balances it and walks out.

About ten minutes later, he returns and goes to the bar. Again, the man asks for a pint and a pork pie. The barman gladly serves him, and the man drinks his pint, picks up his pork pie, puts it on top of this head and walks out with it balanced on his head.

After five minutes, a second man walks into the pub and asks the barman for a pint and a pork pie. The barman replies, "Sorry, we don't have any pork pies left, will a packet of crisps be OK?". The man says 'Sure, a packet of crisps will be fine.'

The second man drinks his pint, then takes the crisps out of the packet and starts balancing them on his head.

Unable to contain his confusion any longer, the barman asks "Excuse me, why are you balancing those crisps on your head?"

The man replies "Because there are no pork pies left!"

16

a

17

c

18

b

Glossary for Chapter 1

apply for	reply to a job advertisement
avalanche victims	people who were killed when stones/snow/mud falls down the side of a mountain
balls	testicles
bat	type of animal, like Batman
check out	consult
crisps	thin slices of fried potatoes typically offered free in pubs
drift	to move with the motion of the sea
figure out	understand
flabbergasted	very surprised
floating	on the surface of the sea
glazed	opaque
grab on	hold
groceries	food that the dog has bought
high-powered	a secretary to someone high in the company hierarchy
hound	synonym for 'dog'
hunter	someone who shoots animals
in awe	very impressed
intrigued	very interested
ladder	used for climbing up and down
landlord	owner of the pub
lawn	grass in front of a house
level crossing	place where a road meets a railway track
meow	sound made by a cat
pass out	faint, go to sleep
paws	dog equivalent of feet
pint	a liquid measurement less than a liter
pit bull	type of violent dog
plank	flat piece of wood
porch	covered space outside front door
pork pie	typical food served in British pubs (pork = pig's meat)
rhinoceros	very large animal

scare	frighten
shake	move quickly
shorthand	a way of writing using symbols instead of words, once frequently used by secretaries and journalists
shot	small glass of strong alcohol
show up	arrive
slide (slid, slid) down	moving down the chair
spring a leak	have a hole in a boat's side that lets the seawater in
squawk	sound made by parrots
steak	portion of meat
suck blood	what a vampire does
take in	absorb information
tank	has two meanings: i) a recipient holding fish ii) an armored vehicle
ten pounds	ten euros, ten dollars
tiniest	very, very small
unconcerned	apparently not worried
unruffled	not worried
wonderment	a mix of surprise and joy

Chapter 2
Doctors

Introduction

There are many kinds of jokes connected with doctors. The most common is the 'Doctor, doctor' joke (jokes 19-28). In 'Doctor, doctor' jokes the context for the joke is immediately set. This means that the joke teller can save time in getting to the point of the joke, the joke is more immediate and easier to remember.

A pattern is followed.

> The jokes are either two lines long or three lines.

> In both cases (2 or 3 lines) the first line is said by the 'patient', and always begins 'doctor, doctor' The patient outlines his or her medical problem. The problem is generally something absurd and is intrinsically funny in itself.

> The second line is said by the doctor. The doctor offers a practical solution to the problem. The solution is generally quite serious and counteracts the absurdity of what has been said by the patient.

> If there is a third line, this is said by the patient, The patient replies to the doctor's suggestion or solution. The patient's reply relates back to his/her initial problem, and is the punch line, i.e. it resolves the whole joke. This punch line usually shows why the doctor's solution cannot work by offering a new perspective on the patient's initial description of the problem.

Below are two examples, the first is a 2-line joke, the second a 3-line joke.

> Doctor, doctor, people keep ignoring me.

> Next!

****

Doctor, doctor, I keep seeing green hairy monsters with hideous faces.
Have you seen a psychologist?
No, just green hairy monsters with hideous faces.

[hideous - very ugly]

Match the beginnings (19-25) with the endings (a-g).

19

Doctor, doctor I have broken my arm in two places.

20

Doctor, doctor, I keep thinking I'm a bell.

21

Doctor, doctor, I keep thinking I'm a set of curtains.

22

Doctor, doctor, I keep thinking I'm invisible.

23

Doctor, doctor, I've only got 59 seconds to live.

24

Doctor, doctor, my husband limps because his left leg is two centimeters shorter than his right leg. What would you do in his case?

25

Doctor, doctor, no one believes a word I say.

- a) Probably limp too.
- b) Pull yourself together man.
- c) Tell me the truth now, what's your real problem?
- d) Wait a minute, please.
- e) Well, just go home and if the feeling persists, give me a ring.
- f) Well, whatever you do, don't go back to those places.
- g) Who said that?

[curtains - material used to stop the light coming through a window; limp - walk with difficulty; pull yourself together - stop complaining. NB: curtains are *pulled in* (or *drawn*) in order to block out the outside. ring - phone call]

Jokes 26-28 are all three liners. However, the doctor's words (the second line) have been removed, and are grouped together (a-c) below the jokes. Insert these second lines into the correct joke.

26

Doctor, doctor, I can't concentrate. One minute I'm OK, and the next minute I go blank.

――――――――――――――――――

What complaint?

27

Doctor, doctor, I keep seeing fish everywhere.

――――――――――――――――――

Look I told you, it's fish that I see.

28

Doctor, doctor, I keep thinking I'm a dog.

――――――――――――――――――

I can't. I'm not allowed on the furniture.

a) Lie down on this couch and I'll examine you.
b) And how long have you had this complaint?
c) Have you seen an optician?

[go blank - totally unable to think and focus; complaint - illness, medical condition; couch - sofa; optician - doctor who tests your eyes]

Match the beginnings and endings (a-f) for jokes 29-34.

a) "I wonder what he meant by that," worried the other.
b) He thought that nobody important was out to get him.
c) The doctor replied, "Until I can come over, write with another pen."
d) The guy answers, "Doc, I'm worried about my brother."
e) The patient sighed, and snapped, "In that case, I'll come back when you're damn well sober!"
f) When she is out of patience.

29

A doctor thoroughly examined his patient, and said, "Look, I really can't find any reason for this mysterious affliction. It's probably due to drinking."

30

When is a doctor most annoyed?

31

A man called his child's doctor, "Hello! My son just snatched my pen when I was writing and swallowed it. What should I do?"

32

Did you hear about the paranoid with low self-esteem?

33

Two psychiatrists walked passed each other in the corridor. "Morning," said one, and nodded.

34

A man walks into the psychiatrist's office with a pancake on his head, fried eggs on each shoulder, and a strip of bacon over each ear. The psychiatrist, humoring him, asks, "What seems to be the problem?"

> [thoroughly - very carefully; affliction - medical condition; annoyed - irritated; nod - move head up and down; pancake, eggs, bacon - food; I wonder what he meant by that - what psychoanalytical analysis did he make about the fact that I said 'morning'? ; come over - come to your house; doc - doctor; snapped - said angrily; sober - not under the influence of alcohol; patience - sounds like 'patients']

In jokes 35 and 36, underline the correct tense.

35

We are back in the 1950s. A woman accompanied her husband to the doctor's office for a checkup. Afterwards, the doctor took the wife aside and said: "Unless you do the following things, your husband *surely dies/will surely die*."

The doctor then went on to say, "Here's what you need to do. Every morning make sure you *serve/will serve* him a good healthy breakfast. Meet him at home each day for lunch so you can serve him a well balanced meal. Make sure you feed him a good, hot meal each evening and *don't/won't* overburden him with any stressful conversation, nor ask him to perform any household chores. Also, keep the house spotless and clean so he *doesn't/won't* get exposed to any threatening germs."

On the way home, the husband asked his wife what the doctor said. She replied, "*You're dying/going to die*."

> [check up - medical examination; well balanced meal - lunch, dinner with the right variation of foodstuffs; overburden - stress; household chores - jobs to do around the house; spotless - very clean and tidy; threatening germs - dangerous micro-organisms causing disease]

36

When Jack and Rick *have met/met* each other on the street one day, Jack noticed that Rick had a terrible cold.

Jack: *Have you seen/Did you see* a doctor about that cold?

Rick: No, but I probably should. *Do you know* a good doctor?

Jack gave him the name of his own doctor and assured him that he *will /would* be in good hands. About a week later, they *have met/met* again and Jack wasn't sure if the cold was really better.

Jack: *Have you seen/Did you see* my doctor?

Rick: Oh, yeah. He was a really nice guy!

Jack: Well, did he give you something to help your cold?

Rick: Sure did! He *has told/told* me to drink a big glass of fresh orange juice after a hot bath.

Jack: Well, did it help?

Rick: How do I know? I haven't even *finished/been finishing* drinking the bath yet!

[be in good hands - be looked after by the right person]

Jokes 37-39 are missing their punch lines.

Below are the punch lines (a-d). Insert them into the correct places.

a) "I suppose I'd just look at my watch."
b) "The bad news is I should have told you that yesterday."
c) "There you are. Of course, if that doesn't work, we'll have to have you put down."

37

At the doctor's office, Tom was getting a check up.
"I have good news and bad news," says the doctor.
"The good news is you have 24 hours left to live."
Tom replies, "That's the good news?!"
Then the doctor says, "_____."

38

A veterinarian was feeling ill and went to see her doctor.
The doctor asked her all the usual questions, about symptoms, how long had they been occurring, etc., when she interrupted him: "Hey look, I'm a vet -- I don't need to ask my patients these kind of questions: I can tell what's wrong just by looking. Why can't you?"

The doctor nodded, looked her up and down, wrote out a prescription, and handed it to her and said: "_____."

39

A man is walking past a hospital for the insane and suddenly remembers an important meeting. Unfortunately, his watch has stopped, and he cannot tell if he is late or not. Then, he notices a patient on the other side of the hospital fence.

Calling out to the patient, the man says, "Pardon me, sir, but do you have the time?"

The patient calls back, "One moment!" and throws himself upon the ground, pulling out a short stick as he does. He pushes the stick into the ground, and, pulling out a carpenter's level, assures himself that the stick is vertical. With a compass, the patient locates north and with a steel ruler, measures the precise length of the shadow cast by the stick. Taking a calculator from his pocket, the patient calculates rapidly, then quickly packs up all his tools and turns back to the pedestrian, saying, "It is now precisely 3:29 pm, provided today is August 16th, which I believe it is."

The man can't help but be impressed by this demonstration, and sets his watch accordingly.

Before he leaves, he says to the patient, "That was really quite remarkable, but tell me, what do you do on a cloudy day, or at night, when the stick casts no shadow?"

The patient holds up his wrist and says: "_____."

> [put down - force to die, like an animal, veterinarian - animal doctor; insane - mentally ill; stick - thin piece of wood; compass - instrument used to understand location; ruler - measuring instrument; shadow - dark shape produced by the sun]

In jokes 40-45 the second line has have been removed. Insert these second lines (a-f) into the correct joke:

a) "$100" replied the dentist. "$100 for a few moments' work?!" exclaimed the patient.
b) "What's the matter with me?" he asks the doctor.
c) The doctor exclaimed, "This is ridiculous! I don't even make that much as a doctor!."
d) His patient looked dubious. "Well, OK." she said, "but would you mind telling me why first?"
e) So she pokes her forearm and screams in pain. Then she touches her thigh and screams again. She pokes her toe and screams.
f) The man says: "I want a second opinion!"

40

A man walks into a doctor's office. He has a cucumber up his nose, a carrot in his left ear and a banana in his right ear.

The doctor replies, "You're not eating properly."

41

A pipe burst in a doctor's house. He called a plumber. The plumber arrived, unpacked his tools, did mysterious plumber-type things for a while, and handed the doctor a bill for $600.

The plumber quietly answered, "Neither did I when I was a doctor."

42

"Would you do me a huge favor and scream in agony a few times?" asked the dentist pleadingly, "I'd really appreciate it."

Oh" he said, "The football's on in an hour and I've got too many patients waiting to stand a chance of making it".

43

"How much will it cost me to have my tooth extracted?" asked the patient.

The dentist smiled and replied: "If you want better value for money, I can extract it very very slowly".

44

A man goes to a psychiatrist. The psychiatrist says: "You're crazy!"

The psychiatrist says: "OK, you are ugly, too!"

45

A woman tells her doctor that her body hurts all over. "Show me," says the doctor.

So she pokes her forearm and screams in pain. Then she touches her thigh and screams again. She pokes her toe and screams.

"I think I know what the problem is," he says. "You have a broken finger." *In jokes 46-48, each joke is followed by three possible punch lines (a, b and c). Choose the punch line which best matches the joke.*

[cucumber - long thin vegetable; burst - broke producing a hole; plumber - expert in water-related problems in the home; making it - being there on time; extract - take out, remove; pokes - pushes; forearm - bottom half of arm; thigh - top half of leg; finger - you have five of these on your hand]

46

A man goes to his doctor for a complete checkup. He hasn't been feeling well and wants to find out if he's ill. After the checkup the doctor comes out with the results of the examination.

"I'm afraid I have some bad news. You're dying and you don't have much time," the doctor says.

"Oh no, that's terrible. How long have I got?" the man asks.

"10..." says the doctor.

"10? 10 what? Months? Weeks? What?!" he asks desperately.

    a) "Ten days"
    b) "10...9...8...7..."
    c) "Tension".

47

A man went to see his doctor because he was suffering from a bad cold. His doctor prescribed some pills, but they didn't help.

On his next visit the doctor gave him a shot, but that didn't do any good.

On his third visit the doctor told the man, "Go home and take a hot bath. As soon as you finish bathing throw open all the windows and stand in the draught."

"But doctor," protested the patient, "if I do that, I'll get pneumonia."

    a) "Who's the doctor round here, me or you?"
    b) "What's pneumonia?"
    c) "I know," said the doctor, "I can cure pneumonia."

[shot - injection; draught - where the wind is; pneumonia - lung inflammation]

48

An inmate went to see the prison doctor and was dismayed to be told that he needed to have one of his kidneys removed.

"Look," said the prisoner, "you've already removed my tonsils, my adenoids, my spleen and my gall-bladder, and now you want my kidney? I only came to you in the first place to see if you could get me out of here!"

The doctor was unruffled.

    a) "And that's exactly what I'm doing," he answered, "bit by bit.
    b) "Do you want to get out of prison or not?"
    c) "Have you dug the tunnel yet?"

[dismayed - unhappy; kidney - internal organ of the body; tonsils, adenoids, spleen, gall bladder - all internal organs; unruffled - not worried; bit by bit - piece by piece; dig the tunnel - make a long hole to escape through]

Key to Chapter 2

19

Doctor, doctor I have broken my arm in two places. Well, whatever you do, don't go back to those places.

20

Doctor, doctor, I keep thinking I'm a bell. Well, just go home and if the feeling persists, give me a ring.

21

Doctor, doctor, I keep thinking I'm a set of curtains. Pull yourself together man.

22

Doctor, doctor, I keep thinking I'm invisible. Who said that?

23

Doctor, doctor, I've only got 59 seconds to live. Wait a minute, please.

24

Doctor, doctor, my husband limps because his left leg is two centimeters shorter than his right leg. What would you do in his case? Probably limp too.

25

Doctor, doctor, no one believes a word I say. Tell me the truth now, what's your real problem?

26

Doctor, doctor, I can't concentrate. One minute I'm OK, and the next minute I go blank.

And how long have you had this complaint?

What complaint?

27

Doctor, doctor, I keep seeing fish everywhere.

Have you seen an optician?

Look I told you, it's fish that I see.

28

Doctor, doctor, I keep thinking I'm a dog.

Lie down on this couch and I'll examine you.

I can't. I'm not allowed on the furniture.

29

A doctor thoroughly examined his patient, and said, "Look, I really can't find any reason for this mysterious affliction. It's probably due to drinking." The patient sighed, and snapped, "In that case, I'll come back when you're damn well sober!"

30

When is a doctor most annoyed? When she is out of patience.

31

A man called his child's doctor, "Hello! My son just snatched my pen when I was writing and swallowed it. What should I do?" The doctor replied, "Until I can come over, write with another pen."

32

Did you hear about the paranoid with low self-esteem? He thought that nobody important was out to get him.

33

Two psychiatrists walked passed each other in the corridor. "Morning," said one, and nodded. "I wonder what he meant by that," worried the other.

34

A man walks into the psychiatrists office with a pancake on his head, fried eggs on each shoulder, and a strip of bacon over each ear. The psychiatrist, humoring him, asks, "What seems to be the problem?" The guy answers, "Doc, I'm worried about my brother."

35

We are back in the 1950s. A woman accompanied her husband to the doctor's office for a checkup. Afterwards, the doctor took the wife aside and said, "Unless you do the following things, your husband *will surely die*." The doctor then went on to say, "Here's what you need to do. Every morning make sure you *serve* him a good healthy breakfast. Meet him at home each day for lunch so you can serve him a well balanced meal. Make sure you feed him a good, hot meal each evening and *don't* overburden him with any stressful conversation, nor ask him to perform any household chores. Also, keep the house spotless and clean so he *doesn't* get exposed to any threatening germs." On the way home, the husband asked his wife what the doctor said. She replied, "You're *going to die*."

36

When Jack and Rick *met* each other on the street one day, Jack noticed that Rick had a terrible cold.

Jack: *Have you seen* a doctor about that cold?

Rick: No, but I probably should. *Do you know* a good doctor?

Jack gave him the name of his own doctor and assured him that *he'd be* in good hands. About a week later, they *met* again and Jack wasn't sure if the cold was really better.

Jack: *Did you see* my doctor?

Rick: Oh, yeah. He was a really nice guy!

Jack: Well, did he give you something to help your cold?

Rick: Sure did! He *told* me to drink a big glass of fresh orange juice after a hot bath.

Jack: Well, did it help?

Rick: How do I know? I haven't even *finished* drinking the bath yet!

37

Then the doctor says, "The bad news is I should have told you that yesterday."

38

The doctor nodded, looked her up and down, wrote out a prescription, and handed it to her and said: "There you are. Of course, if that doesn't work, we'll have to have you put down."

39

The patient holds up his wrist and says, "I suppose I'd just look at my watch."

40

A man walks into a doctor's office. He has a cucumber up his nose, a carrot in his left ear and a banana in his right ear. "What's the matter with me?" he asks the doctor. The doctor replies, "You're not eating properly."

41

A pipe burst in a doctor's house. He called a plumber. The plumber arrived, unpacked his tools, did mysterious plumber-type things for a while, and handed the doctor a bill for $600. The doctor exclaimed, "This is ridiculous! I don't even make that much as a doctor!." The plumber quietly answered, "Neither did I when I was a doctor."

42

"Would you do me a huge favor and scream in agony a few times?" asked the dentist pleadingly, "I'd really appreciate it." His patient looked dubious. "Well, OK." she said, "but would you mind telling me why first?" "Oh" he said, "The football's on in an hour and I've got too many patients waiting to stand a chance of making it".

43

"How much will it cost me to have my tooth extracted?" asked the patient. "$100" replied the dentist. "$100 for a few moments' work?!" exclaimed the patient. The dentist smiled and replied: "If you want better value for money, I can extract it very very slowly".

44

A man goes to a psychiatrist. The psychiatrist says: "You're crazy!" The man says: "I want a second opinion!" The psychiatrist says: "OK, you are ugly, too!"

45

A woman tells her doctor that her body hurts all over. "Show me," says the doctor. So she pokes her forearm and screams in pain. Then she touches her thigh and screams again. She pokes her toe and screams. "I think I know what the problem is," he says. "You have a broken finger."

46

b

47

c

48

a

Glossary for Chapter 2

affliction	medical condition
annoyed	irritated
be in good hands	be looked after by the right person
bit by bit	piece by piece
burst	broke producing a hole
check up	medical examination
come over	come to your house
compass	instrument used to understand location
complaint	illness, medical condition
couch	sofa
cucumber	long thin vegetable
curtains	material used to stop the light coming through a window
dig the tunnel	make a long hole to escape through
dismayed	unhappy
doc	doctor
draught	where the wind is
extract	take out, remove
finger	you have five of these on your hand
forearm	bottom half of arm
go blank	totally unable to think and focus
hideous	very ugly
household chores	jobs to do around the house
insane	mentally ill
kidney	internal organ of the body
limp	walk with difficulty
making it	being there on time
nod	move head up and down
optician	doctor who tests your eyes
overburden	stress
patience	sounds like 'patients'
plumber	expert in water-related problems in the home

pneumonia	lung inflammation
pokes	pushes
pull yourself together	stop complaining
put down	force to die, like an animal, veterinarian animal doctor
ruler	measuring instrument
shadow	dark shape produced by the sun
shot	injection
snapped	said angrily
sober	not under the influence of alcohol
spotless	very clean and tidy
stick	thin piece of wood
thigh	top half of leg
thoroughly	very carefully
threatening germs	dangerous micro-organisms causing disease
unruffled	not worried
well balanced meal	lunch, dinner with the right variation of foodstuffs

Chapter 3
Drunks, Idiots and Husbands

Joke 49 is about three male construction workers and their wives. The joke ends with a comment by each of the three wives. Insert the comments (a, b, c) next to the correct wife.

a) It's so strange because he packs his own lunch.
b) Funny, he never said anything to me.
c) If I had known he didn't want pasta, I would have given him something else.

49

There were three men were working on a big construction platform.

The first man opened his lunchbox and saw a hamburger for his lunch and said: "If I have this stuff one more time, I'll jump off this beam".

The second man looked in his lunchbox and saw pasta and said: "If I have this pasta one more time, I'll jump off this beam".

Then the third man looked into his lunchbox and saw a cheese and tomato sandwich and said: "If I have this sandwich one more time, I'll jump off this beam".

So the next day came and the first man opened his lunchbox and saw a hamburger and promptly jumped off the beam. Then the second man opened his lunchbox and saw pasta and jumped off the beam. So the third man opened his lunchbox and saw cheese and tomato sandwich and he too jumped off the beam.

The three workers' wives showed up at the scene and the workers' boss came over and told them what had happened. He told them that he had overheard the conversation when the three workers were talking about how they were going to jump off the beam if their lunch was the same the next day.

The first man's wife says: _____
The second man's wife: _____

Finally, the third man's wife, who was crying profusely, was barely able to say:

_____

> [packs his own lunch - prepares his lunch and puts it in a container; funny - strange; lunchbox - container for food; beam - long piece of thick metal; profusely - a lot; barely - with difficulty]

In jokes 50-53 the middle line has have been removed. Insert these middle lines (a-d) into the correct joke:

a) "Where have you been?"
b) "Where to?"
c) At Sydney airport, the students catch a cab to their hotel. When they reach their destination, the cabbie says, "That'll be twenty dollars, lads."
d) The boss comes in and says, "What are you doing?"

50

There were two students in London, one gets lost and walks down to the Underground. When they met half an hour later, one says:

_____

"I don't know," replied the other student, "but they had an amazing train set in their cellar".

51

Two very stupid students are traveling to Australia.

Before they leave home, one of their dads gives them both a bit of advice: "You watch them Aussie cab drivers. They'll rob you blind. Don't you go paying them what they ask. You haggle."

_____

"Oh no you don't! My dad warned me about you. You'll only be getting fifteen dollars from me," says one of the students.

"And you'll only be getting fifteen from me too," adds the other.

52

A drunk goes up to the station ticket counter and say: "I want a return ticket."

_____

"Back here you idiot".

53

Two factory workers - a woman and a man - are talking. The woman says, "I can make the boss give me the day off."

The man replies, "And how would you do that?" The woman says, "Just wait and see."

She then hangs upside down from the ceiling.

The woman replies, "I'm a light bulb."

The boss then says, "You've been working so much that you've gone crazy. I think you need to take the day off." The man starts to follow her and the boss says, "Where are you going?"

The man says, "I'm going home, too. I can't work in the dark."

> [cab - taxi; cabbie - taxi driver; lads - boys; underground - train system located underground in a town; train set - model trains; cellar - underground room in a house; Aussie - Australian; haggle - dispute the price and try to get it lower; light bulb - device for providing electric light; day off - a free day from work]

Jokes 54-57 are followed by three possible punch lines (a, b and c). Choose the punch line which best matches the joke.

54

Two drunks were hanging pictures on the walls. One of the drunks started throwing half the nails away.

"Wait a minute," said the friend, "what are you doing that for?"

"Some of the nails have got the heads on the wrong end."

　　a) "Stupid - those are for the other side of the wall."
　　b) "I told you to check the nails at the shop you idiot."
　　c) "What difference does that make?"

> [hang - attach; nail - small piece of metal with pointed end driven into wood or walls to enable something to be attached or joined together]

55

One night a policeman was staking out a pub.

Late in the evening he saw a guy stumble out of the clubhouse and try his keys in five different cars before finding one that opened. Then he sat in the front seat of his car fumbling with his keys for several minutes.

The policeman sat and waited for him to start up, then almost as soon as the man left the car park he pulled the guy over and gave him a breathalyzer test. After asking a few pointless questions and fumbling with the device, the guy blew into the box.

The results showed no alcohol at all.

Puzzled, the policeman made the driver repeat the test, and got the same result – the guy was sober. Worried the policeman offered to fetch Medical assistance if the guy was ill. The guy just smiled at him and said:

    a) "Everything is fine officer. I'm just tonight's designated decoy."
    b) "How did you know I was on medication?"
    c) "I am an actor, I am just practicing being drunk".

[staking out - checking, controlling; stumble out - walk with difficulty probably due to excessive intake of alcohol; fumbling - holding with difficulty; breathalyzer test - test designed to assess level of alcohol in someone's body; device - piece of equipment, in this case the breathalyzer; puzzled - unable to understand; sober - with no traces of alcohol; designated decoy - the person designed to distract the police from seeing the person who really has drunk too much alcohol, the term is a play on the term 'designated driver', who is the one person amongst a group of friends who agrees on this occasion not to drink alcohol so that he/she can drive his/her friends home safely]

56

A proud and confident genius makes a bet with an idiot.

The genius says, "Hey idiot, every question I ask you that you don't know the answer, you have to give me $5. And if you ask me a question and I can't answer yours I will give you $5,000."

The idiot says, "Okay."

The genius then asks, "How many continents are there in the world?"

The idiot doesn't know and hands over the $5.

The idiot says, "Now it's my turn to ask. What animal stands with two legs but sleeps with three?"

The genius tries and searches very hard for the answer but gives up and hands over the $5000.

The genius says, "Damn it, I lost. By the way, what was the answer to your question?"

The idiot hands over $5.

The idiot says:

    a) "Well I suppose that's why people call me an idiot".
    b) "A walking stick is not exactly a third leg".
    c) "I thought you were supposed to be the genius" and runs off with the money".

57

Two senile old men were out fishing in the middle of a lake in a rented boat. They had been doing particularly well, catching fish after fish, all well above the average size. At the end of the day they rowed ashore very pleased with themselves. "That was the best spot where I have ever fished," commented one of them. "I hope you marked it in some way so that we can go back."

"Oh, I have," his friend replied. 'I put an X on the side of the boat."

"That's no good," the other replied, "… "

    a) the fish may have moved to a different spot next time
    b) we may not get the same boat next time
    c) what happens if we decide to go out at night?

[spot - location; marked - noted with a physical sign;]

Decide whether in the following jokes (58-63), the butt (i.e. the focus of fun) of the joke is

    a) *the husband*
    b) *the wife.*
    c) *both the husband and the wife*

58

On a particular warm day one summer, a man decided to sunbathe naked in his back garden. Having recently built a large fence he was confident that no one would be able to see him.

"I wonder," he said to his wife, "what the neighbors would say if they could see me".

"They'd probably say that I must have married you for the money", replied his wife.

59

A woman was telling her friend about the tragic and sudden death of her husband.

"One minute he was with me and then he went out into the garden to pick some peas for our dinner and he dropped dead," she said.

"That's terrible," said her friend. "What did you do?"

"I opened a tin of beans instead," she replied.

> [peas and beans are both vegetables]

60

A middle aged woman goes to visit a fortune teller.

"I see only good for you," says the fortune teller. "You will meet a tall dark handsome stranger who will sweep you off your feet and make you incredibly happy".

"That's great" says the woman, "just one question though, what'll happen to my husband?"

> [fortune teller - someone who predicts your future; sweep you off your feet - make you fall in love with him]

61

A husband and wife were very happy when finally their long wait to adopt a baby had come to an end. The adoption center called and told them they had a wonderful Russian baby boy. The couple agreed to take the baby without hesitation. On the way home from the adoption center, they stopped by the local college so they each could enroll in night courses.

After they filled out the form, the registration clerk inquired, "Why do you want to study Russian?"

The couple said proudly, "We just adopted a Russian baby and in a year or so he'll start to talk. We just want to be able to understand him."

62

A wife sends her husband an sms on a cold winter evening: "Windows frozen".

The husband sends his answer back: "Pour some warm water over them".

Some time later the husband receives answer from his wife:

"The computer is completely bust now".

> [Windows - computer operating system, but also what the natural light comes through in a house; frozen - not working (in the case of software], covered in ice (in the case of a meteorological event); bust - broken (because the wife has put water on the computer)]

63

A guy walked into a barbershop and asked: "How long before I can get a haircut?"

The barber looked around the shop full of customers and said, "About 2 hours."

The guy left.

A few days later, the same guy stuck his head in the door and asked, "How long before I can get a haircut?"

The barber looked around at the shop and said, "About 3 hours."

The guy left.

A week later, the same guy stuck his head in the shop and asked, "How long before I can get a haircut?"

The barber looked around the shop and said, "About an hour and a half."

The guy left.

The barber turned to his friend and said, "Hey, Jack, do me a favor, follow him and see where he goes. He keeps asking how long he has to wait for a haircut, but he never comes back."

A little while later, Jack returned to the shop, laughing hysterically.

The barber asked, "So, where does he go when he leaves?"

Jack looked up, still laughing, and said: "To your house!"

> [barbershop - place where a man has his hair cut; barber - man who cuts hair]

Key to Chapter 3

49

The first man's wife says: Funny, he never said anything to me."

The second man's wife: If I had known he didn't want pasta I would have given him something else."

Finally, the third man's wife, who was crying profusely, was barely able to say: "It's so strange because he packs his own lunch."

50

There were two students in London, one gets lost and walks down to the Underground. When they met half an hour later, one says: *"Where have you been?"* "I don't know," replied the other student, "but they had an amazing train set in their cellar".

51

Two very stupid students are traveling to Australia. Before they leave home, one of their dads gives them both a bit of advice: "You watch them Aussie cab drivers. They'll rob you blind. Don't you go paying them what they ask. You haggle." *At the Sydney airport, the students catch a cab to their hotel. When they reach their destination, the cabbie says, "That'll be twenty dollars, lads."* "Oh no you don't! My dad warned me about you. You'll only be getting fifteen dollars from me," says one of the students. "And you'll only be getting fifteen from me too," adds the other.

52

A drunk goes up to the station ticket counter and say: "I want a return ticket." *"Where to?"* "Back here you idiot".

53

Two factory workers - a woman and a man - are talking. The woman says, "I can make the boss give me the day off." The man replies, "And how would you do that?" The woman says, "Just wait and see." She then hangs upside down from the ceiling. *The boss comes in and says, "What are you doing?"* The woman replies, "I'm a light bulb." The boss then says, "You've been working so much that you've gone crazy. I think you need to take the day off." The man starts to follow her and the boss says, "Where are you going?" The man says, "I'm going home, too. I can't work in the dark."

Key to Chapter 3

54

a

55

a

56

c (The genius hands over the $5000 without getting an answer; so in reality the genius is an idiot, and the idiot is a genius).

57

b

58

Husband

59

Husband

60

Husband

61

Husband and wife

62

Wife and husband?

63

Husband?

Glossary for Chapter 3

Aussie	Australian
barber	man who cuts hair
barbershop	place where a man has his hair cut
barely	with difficulty
beam	long piece of thick metal
breathalyzer test	test designed to assess level of alcohol in someone's body
bust	broken (because the wife has put water on the computer)
cab	taxi
cabbie	taxi driver
cellar	underground room in a house
day off	a free day from work
device	piece of equipment, in this case the breathalyzer
fortune teller	someone who predicts your future
frozen	not working (in the case of software, covered in ice (in the case of a meteorological event)
fumbling	holding with difficulty
funny	strange
haggle	dispute the price and try to get it lower
hang	attach
lads	boys
light bulb	device for providing electric light
lunchbox	container for food
marked	noted with a physical sign
nail	small piece of metal with pointed end driven into wood or walls to enable something to be attached or joined together
profusely	a lot
puzzled	unable to understand
sober	with no traces of alcohol
spot	location
stake out	check, control

stumble out	walk with difficulty probably due to excessive intake of alcohol
sweep you off your feet	make you fall in love
train set	model trains
underground	train system located underground in a town

Chapter 4
Knock Knock

Introduction

A 'knock knock' is a five-line joke where the teller of the joke interacts with the listener. It has the following formula:

> Line 1: The teller of the joke says "Knock knock", imagining that they are knocking at the door of someone's house.
> Line 2: The listener, who imagines that they are inside the house, automatically replies "Who's there?"
> Line 3: The teller says the first name of a person.
> Line 4: The listener automatically repeats the first name of the person plus *who*, indicating that they want to know the surname.
> Line 5: This is the punch line. The teller replies not by saying the surname but by saying something that 'plays' on the sound of first name that they said in Line 3.

This may seem complicated, so let's look at some examples.

> Knock, knock.
> Who's there?
> Harry. [*first name of a person*]
> Harry who? [*first name + who*]
> Harry up, it's cold out here! [*play on the sound of the name Harry*]

In the above case *Harry up* sounds like *Hurry up* (i.e. be quick).

> Knock, knock.
> Who's there?
> Isabel.
> Isabel who?
> Isabel necessary on a bicycle?

In this case Isabel sounds like *Is a bell*, meaning does a bicycle need to have a bell on it.

Although the original Knock Knock jokes always made use of a first name, they are now often used with any word which when pronounced quickly sounds like another word or phrase.

Sometimes Knock Knock jokes come in different formats:

> Knock, knock.
> Who's there?
> Army.
> Army who?
> Army and you still friends? [*Are you and me* still friends]

Essentially, in order to tell (and understand) a Knock Knock joke, you need to try and say the name that appears in the third line very quickly when you say it in the fifth line.

Note: In some part of the English speaking world, people don't always pronounce the TH sound correctly. This means that TH can pronounced like an F or D. Some non-native speakers also replace the TH sound with a Z sound. For example *fink* (instead of *think*), *day* (instead of *they*) and *zat* (instead of *that*).

To prepare yourself for reading the jokes, do the following exercises, and then check with the key at the end of the chapter.

Match the names (a-i) with words and phrases (1-9).

a) Abby
b) Aida
c) Alex
d) Althea
e) Arthur (pronounced Arfur in Essex, England)
f) Ben
g) Dave
h) Iona
i) Iva

1. Happy
2. I for
3. I had a
4. I have a
5. I have been
6. I own a
7. I will (ex)
8. I will see you
9. They've

Match the names (k-r) with words and phrases

j) Ivor
k) Justin
l) Luke
m) Nana
n) Noah
o) Norma Lee
p) Sadie
q) Sarah
r) Watson

10. Either
11. I'm just in
12. Look
13. It's none of
14. Do you know a
15. Normally
16. Say the
17. Is there a
18. What's on

For jokes 64-81, try to understand the meaning of the last line. The best solution is to true to read the word quite quickly and hear what other word or combination of words it sounds like.

64

Knock, knock.
Who's there?
Abby.
Abby who?
Abby birthday!

65

Knock, knock.
Who's there?
Aida.
Aida who?
Aida sandwich for lunch today.

66

Knock, knock
Who's there?
Alex.
Alex who?
Alex plain later!

67

Knock, knock.
Who's there?
Althea.
Althea who?
Althea later!

68

Knock, knock.
Who's there?
Arthur.
Arthur who?
Arthur got!

69

Knock, knock
Who's there?
Ben.
Ben who?
Ben knocking for 10 minutes.

70

Knock knock!
Who's there?
Dave
Dave who?
Dave locked me out again.

71

Knock, knock.
Who's there?
Iona.
Iona who?
Iona new car!

72

Knock, knock
Who's there?
Iva.
Iva who?
Iva sore hand from knocking!

73

Knock, knock.
Who's there?
Ivor.
Ivor who?
Ivor you let me in or I'll climb through the window

74

Knock, knock.
Who's there?
Justin
Justin who?
Justin time for dinner!

75

Knock, knock.
Who's there?
Luke.
Luke who?
Luke through the the peep hole and find out.

76

Knock, knock.
Who's there?
Nana.
Nana who?
Nana your business.

77

Knock, knock.
Who's there?
Noah.
Noah who?
Noah good place we can get something to eat?

78

Knock, knock.
Who's there?
Norma Lee.
Norma Lee who?
Norma Lee I don't go around knocking on doors, but I just had to meet you!

79

Knock, knock
Who's there?
Sadie.
Sadie who?
Sadie magic word and watch me disappear!

80

Knock knock!
Who's there?
Sarah
Sarah who?
Sarah doctor in the house?

81

Knock, knock!
Who's there?
Watson.
Watson who?
Watson TV tonight?

For jokes 82-89, try to understand what the first word of the last line means. The best solution is to true to read the word quite quickly and hear what other word or combination of words it sounds like.

If you have difficulty, try to match the words and phrases below with the first word of the last line.

a) Aren't you ...
b) Can you ...
c) Check in ...
d) Doesn't ...
e) Fix ...
f) Haven't you ...
g) I need a ...
h) Is there any ...

Note: The words in the third line have a totally unconnected meaning with the joke - it is only their sound that is important. Here are some brief definitions:

> avenue - a road line with trees; canoe - small, narrow boat; chicken - bird raised for its eggs and meat; dozen - another word for 'twelve'; figs - a fruit; lettuce - a vegetable; needle - small very thin rod of metal used for sewing; nobel - as in Nobel Prize; orange - color, fruit; zany - strange

82

Knock, knock.
Who's there?
Avenue.
Avenue who?
Avenue knocked on this door before?

83

Knock, knock.
Who's there?
Canoe.
Canoe who?
Canoe help me with my homework?

84

Knock, knock.
Who's there?
Chicken.
Chicken who?
Chicken your pockets. I think the keys are in there.

85

Knock, knock.
Who's there?
Dozen.
Dozen who?
Dozen anybody want to let me in?

86

Knock, knock.
Who's there?
Figs
Figs who?
Figs the doorbell, it's broken!

87

Knock, knock.
Who's there?
Needle.
Needle who?
Needle little money for the movies.

88

Knock, knock.
Who's there?
Orange.
Orange who?
Orange you going to let me in?

89

Knock, knock.
Who's there?
Zany
Zany who?
Zany body home?

Try to understand what the first word of the last line means. The best solution is to true to read the word quite quickly and hear what other word or combination of words it sounds like.

If you have difficulty, try to match the words and phrases below with the first word of the last line.

    a) (Do) you see
    b) Catch up
    c) I bet
    d) Let us ...
    e) Please
    f) There's no bell ...
    g) This is
    h) Wipe her

90

Knock, knock.
Who's there?
Police.
Police who?
Police hurry up, it's chilly outside!

91

Knock, knock!
Who's there?
Ketchup.
Ketchup who?
Ketchup with me and I'll tell you!

92

Knock, knock.
Who's there?
Dishes.
Dishes who?
Dishes a nice place!

93

Knock, knock.
Who's there?
CD.
CD who?
CD guy on your doorstep?

94

Knock, knock.
Who's there?
Abbot.
Abbot who?
Abbot you don't know who this is!

95

Knock, knock.
Who's there?
Viper.
Viper who?
Viper nose, it's running!

96

Knock, knock.
Who's there?
"Nobel."
"Nobel who?"
"No bell that's why I knocked."

97

Knock, knock.
Who's there?
Lettuce.
Lettuce who?
Lettuce in. It's cold outside.

This last set of Knock Knock jokes (98-104) is a variation on the traditional version. There is no name of a person, and the word used in the third line is not replicated in the fifth line. Instead the last line is used as a reaction to the fourth line. Read the jokes and see if you can understand the connection between the fourth and fifth lines.

98

Knock, knock.
Who's there?
Ya.
Ya who?
Wow. You sure are excited to see me!

99

Knock, knock.
Who's there?
Cows go
Cows go who?
Cows don't go who, they go moo!

100

Knock, knock.
Who's there?
Etch.
Etch who?
Bless you!

101

Knock, knock.
Who's there?
I am.
I am who?
You mean you don't know who you are?

102

Knock, knock.
Who's there?
Tank.
Tank who?
Your welcome!

103

Knock, knock!
Who's there?
Spell.
Spell who?
W-H-O

104

Will you remember me in two minutes?
Yes.
Knock, knock.
Who's there?
Hey, you didn't remember me!

Key to Chapter 4

Abby - Happy

Aida - I had a

Alex - I will (ex)

Althea - I will see you

Arthur (pronounced Arfur in Essex, England) = I for

Ben - I have been

Dave - They've

Iona - I own a

Iva - I have a

Ivor - Either

Justin - I'm just in

Luke - Look

Nana - It's none of

Noah - Do you know a

Norma Lee - Normally

Sadie - Say the

Sarah - Is there a

Watson - What's on

64-81

Abby - Happy birthday

Aida - I had a sandwich for lunch today

Alex - I will explain later

Althea - I will see you later

Arthur - I forgot

Ben - I have been knocking for 10 minutes

Dave - They've locked me out again

Iona - I own a new car

Iva - I have a sore hand from knocking

Ivor - Either you let me in or I'll climb through the window

Justin - Just in time for dinner

Luke - Look through the the peep hole and find out

Nana - It's none of your business

Noah - Do you know a good place we can get something to eat

Norma Lee - Normally

Sadie - Say the magic word and watch me disappear

Sarah - Is there a doctor in the house

Watson - What's on TV tonight

82-89

Avenue knocked on this door before? = Haven't you …

Canoe help me with my homework? = Can you …

Chicken your pockets. I think the keys are in there. = Check in …

Dozen anybody want to let me in? = Doesn't …

Figs the doorbell, it's broken! = Fix …

Needle little money for the movies. = I need a …

Orange you going to let me in? = Aren't you …

Zany body home? Is there any …

90-97

Police hurry up, it's chilly outside! = Please

Ketchup with me and I'll tell you! = Catch up

Dishes a nice place! = This is

CD guy on your doorstep? = (Do) you see

Abbot you don't know who this is! = I bet

Viper nose, it's running! = Wipe her

Nobel that's why I knocked. = There's no bell …

Lettuce in. It's cold outside. = Let us …

98

Ya who? = Yahoo (an exclamation of joy and excitement)

99

Cows go who? = in the formula of Knock Knock jokes, the listener always repeats the name given by the teller in the third line, in this case *cows go*. The verb *to go* is also used when we want to imitate the sound that an animal makes. So for a dog or cat we would say *a dog goes 'bow wow'*, or *a cat goes 'miaow'*. But a cow obviously doesn't go *who* but *moo*.

Key to Chapter 4 55

100

The sound that we make when sneezing is *aah choo*, which sounds very similar to *etch who*. When someone sneezes then a typical reaction is to say *Bless you*. The word *etch* has nothing to do with the joke, it means to engrave and is a term used in art.

101

I am who? = Gives the idea that the speaker doesn't know who he/she is.

102

Tank who? = thank you

103

Spell who? = Please can you spell the word *who* to me.

104

Self explanatory.

Glossary for Chapter 4

avenue a road line with trees
canoe small, narrow boat
chicken bird raised for its eggs and meat
dozen another word for 'twelve'
figs a fruit
lettuce a vegetable
needle small very thin rod of metal used for sewing
nobel as in Nobel Prize
orange color, fruit
zany strange

Chapter 5
Professions

Joke 105 recounts a conversation between <u>three</u> professionals. Below is a list of five professionals (a-e). Decide which three of the five professionals are the protagonist of the joke and insert them into the appropriate places.

a) *architect*
b) *computer programmer*
c) *engineer*
d) *lawyer*
e) *manager*

105

There was an _____, a _____ and a _____ driving down a steep hill. The brakes failed, and the car careered down the road out of control. Half way down the driver managed to stop the car by running it against a hedge narrowly avoiding going over a cliff. They all got out, shaken by their narrow escape from death, but otherwise unharmed.

The _____ said: "To fix this problem we need to organize a committee, have meetings, and through a process of continuous improvement, develop a solution."

The _____ said: "No that would take too long, and besides that method never worked before. I have my pen knife here and will take apart the brake system, isolate the problem and correct it."

The _____ said: "You're both wrong! We should push the car back up the hill and see if it happens again."

[steep - going down (up) sharply; brakes - mechanical device to stop the car moving; failed - didn't work; career - move very rapidly with no control; unharmed - with no injuries; committee - group of people with a designated task to resolve; pen knife - small knife for multiple uses]

Insert the right job (a-e) into the spaces in jokes 106 and 107.

a) chemist
b) engineer
c) physicist
d) programmer
e) statistician

106

Three professors - a _____ , a _____ , and a _____ - are called in to see the dean of their university. Just as they arrive the dean is called out of his office, leaving the three professors there. The professors see with alarm that there is a fire in the wastebasket.

The _____ says: "I know what to do! We must cool down the materials until their temperature is lower than the ignition temperature and then the fire will go out."

The _____ says: "No! No! I know what to do! We must cut off the supply of oxygen so that the fire will go out due to lack of one of the reactants."

While the _____ and _____ debate what course to take, they both are alarmed to see the _____ running around the room starting other fires. They both scream: "What are you doing?"

To which the _____ replies: "Trying to get an adequate sample size."

[dean - head of a university faculty; wastebasket - recipient for trash; cut off - terminate; lack - absence; sample size - the number of individual pieces of data collected in a survey]

107

An _____ , a _____ , and a _____ were in a car driving over a steep alpine pass when the brakes failed. The car was getting faster and faster, they were struggling to get round the corners and once or twice only the feeble crash barrier saved them from crashing down the side of the mountain. They were sure they were all going to die, when suddenly they spotted an escape lane. They pulled into the escape lane, and came safely to a halt.

The _____ said "We need to model the friction in the brake pads and the resultant temperature rise, see if we can work out why they failed".

The _____ said "I think I've got a few spanners in the back. I'll take a look and see if I can work out what's wrong".

The _____ said "Why don't we get going again and see if it's reproducible?"

[Note: This is a variation of joke 105, so the concepts are very similar.]

Decide which of the three punch lines (a, b, c) is the best ending for the following jokes.

108

At the station, three accountants each buy tickets and watch as three engineers buy only a single ticket.

"How are three people going to travel on only one ticket?" asks one of the accountants.

"Watch and you'll see," answers one of the engineers. All of them board the train.

The accountants take their respective seats but all three engineers cram into a restroom and close the door behind them.

Shortly after the train has departed, the conductor comes around collecting tickets. He knocks on the restroom door and says, "Ticket, please." The door opens just a crack and a single arm emerges with a ticket in hand. The conductor takes it and moves on.

The accountants saw this and agreed it was a clever idea. So after the conference, the accountants decide to copy the engineers on the return trip and save some money.

When they get to the station they buy a single ticket for the return trip. To their astonishment, the engineers don't buy a ticket at all.

"How are you going to travel without a ticket?" says one perplexed accountant.

"Watch and you'll see," answers an engineer.

When they board the train the three accountants cram into a restroom and the three engineers cram into another one nearby.

The train departs. Shortly afterward, one of the engineers leaves his restroom and walks over to the restroom where the accountants are hiding. He knocks on the door and says:

    a) "Ticket, please."
    b) "This is the ticket inspector. Please show your ticket please."
    c) "You're on the wrong train."

[accountant - someone who deals with financial records; cram into - fit into a small space; restroom - bathroom; conductor - inspector of tickets; perplexed - confused; hiding - trying not to be seen]

109

One day, a Mechanical Engineer, an Electrical Engineer, a Chemical Engineer and a Computer Engineer were driving down the street in the same car. All of a sudden, the car broke down.

The Mechanical Engineer said, "I think a rod broke."

The Chemical Engineer said, "The way it sputtered at the end, I don't think it's getting gas."

The Electrical Engineer said, "I think there was a spark and something is wrong with the electrical system." All three turned to the computer engineer and said, "What do you think?"

The Computer Engineer said:

a) "I think we should all get out and get back in."
b) "Windows are down - try winding them up."
c) "Let's look in the manual."

[rod - a mechanical part of the engine; sputtered - made a series of soft explosive sounds; gas - gasoline, petrol; spark - spark(ing) plug = device for firing the explosive mixture in an engine]

In jokes 110, 111 and 112, a sentence has been removed. Choose the most appropriate sentence (a-f) to fill the gaps. Note: You only need three of the sentence.

a) "What's your name?"
b) "Wow, that was the shortest runway I've ever seen!"
c) "But I'm a college graduate"
d) "How long is a piece of string?"
e) "Where's the broom?"
f) "We're lucky to be alive."

110

A young man hired by a supermarket reported for his first day of work. The manager greeted him with a warm handshake and a smile, gave him a broom and said, "Your first job will be to sweep out the store."

"_____" the young man replied indignantly.

"Oh, I'm sorry. I didn't know that," said the manager. "Here, give me the broom – I'll show you how."

111

At the top-secret army headquarters, two generals were testing the new speaking computer. They asked the computer a question: "_____" "

After a few moments the computer replied "five thousand".

"Five thousand what?" asked one of the generals.

"Five thousand, sir" replied the computer.

112

An airplane lands with great difficulty, stopping just short of an accident.

When they arrive at the gate, the captain wipes his brow and says: "_____"

"You're not kidding," says his co-pilot, looking out of the window. "But it sure is wide".

[runway - the strip of land at an airport where the planes land; string - twisted cotton or other material for tying things with; broom - brush; sweep - the action of cleaning using a brush; wipe his brow - remove the sweat from the top half of his face; kidding - joking]

For joke 113, choose the correct tense.

113

There was an engineer who *had/had had* an exceptional gift for fixing anything mechanical. After serving his company loyally for over 30 years, he happily *retired*.

Several years later the company *contacted/were contacting* him regarding a seemingly impossible problem they *had/were having* with one of their multi-million dollar machines. They *tried/had tried* everything and everyone else to get the machine fixed, but to no avail.

In desperation, they *called/had called* on the retired engineer who *solved/had solved* so many of their problems in the past. The engineer reluctantly took the challenge. He spent a day studying the huge machine.

At the end of the day, he marked a small "x" in chalk on a particular component of the machine and proudly stated, "This is where your problem is".

The part *was replaced/had replaced* and the machine *worked/had worked* perfectly again. The company *received/were receiving* a bill for $50,000 from the engineer for his service.

They demanded an itemized accounting of his charges.

The engineer responded briefly:

One chalk mark: $1

Knowing where to put it: $49,999

[retire - stop working because you reach a certain age; loyally - without ever changing company; seemingly - apparently; to no avail - without success; reluctantly - without really wanting to; challenge - difficult task; chalk - material usually used for writing on a blackboard; itemized accounting - a list of all the things he had done plus the relevant costs; charges - the amounts he wanted the company to pay him]

The next two jokes (114 and 115) are about people with an MBA - a Master's of Business Administration (MBA). Such people tend to earn very large amounts of money working for consultancy firms. They also have a reputation for thinking that they are more intelligent than most other people.

The seven paragraphs in the joke below are in the wrong order. Put them in the right order.

114

Always looking to show off his MBA skills, he bets the shepherd he could determine exactly how many sheep are in the flock. If he is right, the graduate gets one sheep. The shepherd agrees.

The MBA graduate goes back to his car, fires up his GPS, laptop and cell phone. He gets a detailed satellite picture of their exact location, downloads the picture and uses grid technology to count the exact number of sheep.

The shepherd replies: "You showed the three tell tale signs of all consultants. First, you showed up here without being asked or invited. Second, I paid you to tell me something I already knew. Last, you know absolutely nothing about my business because you just put my dog in your car."

A graduate with an MBA goes on vacation to the Australian outback. In his travels he comes across a sheep herder with a huge flock. He stops his car, approaches the shepherd and introduces himself.

After only a few minutes the graduate walks up to the shepherd and tells him he has 3,766 sheep. The shepherd confirms the number and the proud graduate loads an animal into his car.

The amazed graduate confirms this and asks the shepherd how he knew.

Before the graduate can drive away, the shepherd approaches the car and offers to bet him double or nothing that he could guess the graduate's profession. The graduate agrees. The shepherd tells him that he is a consultant.

[shepherd/sheep herder - someone who looks after sheep; fires up his GPS - gets his geographical positioning system device ready; showed up - arrive unexpectedly; bet him double or nothing - a gamble to decide whether a debt should be doubled or canceled]

Read joke 115 and then decide whether the last line really is the last line, or whether the punch line is missing.

115

An American tourist was on vacation on a very small Greek island. A fishing boat docked in the harbor and the tourist complimented the Greek fisherman on the quality of his fish and asked how long it had taken him to catch them.

"Not very long," answered the Greek.

"Then why didn't you stay out longer and catch more?" asked the American.

The Greek explained that his small catch was sufficient to meet his needs and those of his customers.

The American asked, "But what do you do with the rest of your time?"

"I sleep late, fish a little, play with my children, and take a siesta with my wife. In the evenings I go into the village to see my friends, dance a little, and sing a few songs. I have a full life."

The American interrupted, "I have an MBA and I can help you. You should start by fishing longer every day. You can sell the extra fish you catch. With the revenue, you can buy a bigger boat, catch even more fish. With the extra money you will soon be able to buy a second one and a third one and so on until you have an entire fleet of trawlers. Instead of selling your fish to a middleman, you can negotiate directly with the processing plants and maybe even open your own plant. You can then leave this little village and move to Athens, Los Angeles, or even New York City! From there you can direct your huge enterprise."

"How long would that take?" asked the Greek

"Twenty, perhaps twenty-five years," replied the American.

"And after that?"

"After that you'll be able to retire, live in a tiny village near the sea, sleep late, fish a little, play with your grandchildren, take a siesta with your wife, and spend your evenings in the village, dancing and singing with your friends."

[docked - attached by a rope to the land; fleet of trawlers - a lot of fishing boats; middleman - intermediary; enterprise - business]

Decide which of the three punch lines (a, b, c) is the best ending for jokes 116 and 117.

116

A local charity realized that it had never received a donation from the town's most successful lawyer.

The person in charge of contributions called the lawyer to persuade her to contribute. "Our research shows that out of a yearly income of at least $500,000, you did not give a penny to charity. Wouldn't you like to give back to the community in some way?"

The lawyer mulled this over for a moment and replied, "First, did your research also show that my mother is dying after a long illness, and has medical bills that are several times her annual income?"

Embarrassed, the contribution manager mumbled, "Um, no."

The lawyer interrupts, "Or that my brother, a disabled veteran, is blind and confined to a wheelchair?"

The contribution manager began to stammer out an apology, but was interrupted again.

"Or that my sister's husband died in a traffic accident," the lawyer's voice rising in indignation, "leaving her penniless with three children?!"

The humiliated contribution manager, completely beaten, said simply, "I had no idea."

On a roll, the lawyer cut him off once again,

    a) "So if I don't give any money to them, why should I give any to you?"
    b) "So you can understand why I don't wish to give any money to you.
    c) "So if you just let me get my checkbook I'll make you out a big check"

[charity - non-profit organization set up to help people in need; donation - money; penny - cent (very small amount of money); mull over - think about, reflect on; income - money received through work or investment; mumble - say unclearly; veteran - someone who has fought in a war; blind - unable to say; penniless - with no money; on a roll - experiencing a prolonged period of success; cut off - stop someone from talking; beaten - lost the battle to convince the lawyer to contribute; check (GB: cheque) - a piece of paper with a sum of money written on it that the receiver can reclaim at a bank]

117

One afternoon, a wealthy lawyer was riding in the back of his limousine when he saw two men eating grass by the roadside. He ordered his driver to stop and he got out to investigate.

"Why are you eating grass," he asked one man?

"We don't have any money for food," the poor man replied.

"Oh, well, you can come with me to my house", instructed the lawyer.

"But, sir, I have a wife and two children with me!"

"Bring them along!" said the lawyer.

He turned to the other man and said, "You come with us, too."

"But, sir, I have a wife and six children!" he answered.

"Bring them as well! " answered the lawyer as he headed for his limo.

Once underway, one of the poor fellows said: "Sir, you are too kind. Thank you for taking all of us with you."

The lawyer replied:

> a) "It's OK, I'll get my secretary to send you a bill for the cost of the gasoline."
> b) "Glad to do it. You'll love my place; the grass is almost a foot high!"
> c) "That's fine, in fact if you like you can all come and work for me."

[wealthy - rich; limousine - long luxurious car; almost a foot high - around 30 cm in height]

Below are eight paragraphs from two jokes (118 and 119) that have been mixed up. Each joke has four paragraphs. See if you can recreate the two jokes.

Joke 118 : ____ _____ _____ _____

Joke 119 : ____ _____ _____ _____

118 and 119

1) After an hour of this, the exasperated doctor asks the lawyer, "What do you do to stop people from asking you for legal advice when you're out of the office?"
2) "But it's only $500," replied the man. "Precisely. That's what he will reply and then you'll have your proof!"
3) "Do you have any proof he owes you the money?" asked the lawyer. "Nope," replied the man.
4) "I give it to them," replies the lawyer, "and then I send them a bill."

5) "OK, then write him a letter asking him for the $5,000 he owed you," said the lawyer.
6) A doctor and a lawyer are talking at a party. Their conversation is constantly interrupted by people describing their ailments and asking the doctor for free medical advice.
7) A man went to his lawyer and asked him, "My neighbor owes me $500 and he won't pay up. What should I do?"
8) The doctor is shocked, but agrees to give it a try. The next day, still feeling slightly guilty, the doctor prepares the bills. When he goes to place them in his mailbox, he finds a bill from the lawyer.

[exasperated - frustrated; proof - demonstration; ailments - medical conditions; owes - to be in debt with someone; give it a try - make an attempt; guilty - the opposite of innocent]

Match the jokes (120-124) to their punch lines (a-f). Note there are only four jokes, but six possible punch lines.

a) He threatened to release one every hour if his demands weren't met.
b) I don't have to, I only have to outrun you.
c) I suppose so. What's you third question?
d) No but I can represent you when you take legal action against him.
e) Oh my god! Where is my Rolex!?
f) Well, at least I can claim a new arm on insurance.
g) That's all true, but I got the voltage lowered.

120

Lawyer: "I have some good news for you"

Client: "What good news? You lost my case, I was convicted of a murder I did not commit and was sentenced to die in the electric chair".

Lawyer: _____

121

Two lawyers walking through the woods spotted a vicious looking bear.

The first lawyer immediately opened her briefcase, pulled out a pair of sneakers and started putting them on.

The second lawyer looked at her and said, "You're crazy! You'll never be able to outrun that bear!"

First lawyer: _____

122

A lawyer opens the door of his BMW. Suddenly, a passing car hits the door and it flies away. The lawyer gets so mad – she loves her BMW so much! Soon, the police arrive.

The lawyer exclaims: "Officer, look what happened to my BMW!"

"Lawyers are so materialistic!" says the officer, "You are worried about your stupid BMW! Didn't you notice you're missing your left arm?"

And the lawyer replies: _____

123

A man calls his lawyer and asks: "How much would you charge me to answer three questions"

The lawyer replies: "Four hundred dollars.

The man retorts: "That's a bit steep don t you think?"

And the lawyer replies: _____

124

Did you hear about the terrorist that hijacked an airplane full of lawyers?

_____

[lose a case - when a lawyer's client is found to be guilty; to sentence - to assign someone a punishment; sneakers - shoes; outrun - run faster than; mad - angry; to charge - request a certain amount of money for a service; a bit steep - too expensive; hijacked - illegally take over an aircraft or other vehicle via force]

Key to Chapter 5

105

There was an engineer, a manager and a computer programmer driving down a steep hill. The brakes failed and the car careered down the road out of control. Half way down the driver managed to stop the car by running it against a hedge narrowly avoiding going over a cliff. They all got out, shaken by their narrow escape from death, but otherwise unharmed.

The manager said "To fix this problem we need to organize a committee, have meetings, and through a process of continuous improvement, develop a solution."

The engineer said "No that would take too long, and besides that method never worked before. I have my trusty pen knife here and will take apart the brake system, isolate the problem and correct it."

The programmer said "You're both wrong! We should push the car back up the hill and see if it happens again."

106

Three professors - a *physicist*, a *chemist* and a *statistician* - are called in to see the dean of their university. Just as they arrive the dean is called out of his office, leaving the three professors there. The professors see with alarm that there is a fire in the wastebasket.

The *physicist* says, "I know what to do! We must cool down the materials until their temperature is lower than the ignition temperature and then the fire will go out."

The *chemist* says, "No! No! I know what to do! We must cut off the supply of oxygen so that the fire will go out due to lack of one of the reactants."

While the *physicist* and *chemist* debate what course to take, they both are alarmed to see the *statistician* running around the room starting other fires. They both scream, "What are you doing?"

To which the *statistician* replies, "Trying to get an adequate sample size."

107

An *engineer*, a *physicist*, and a *programmer* were in a car driving over a steep alpine pass when the brakes failed. The car was getting faster and faster, they were struggling to get round the corners and once or twice only the feeble crash barrier saved them from crashing down the side of the mountain. They were sure they were all going to die, when suddenly they spotted an escape lane. They pulled into the escape lane, and came safely to a halt.

The *physicist* said "We need to model the friction in the brake pads and the resultant temperature rise, see if we can work out why they failed".

The *engineer* said "I think I've got a few spanners in the back. I'll take a look and see if I can work out what's wrong".

The *programmer* said "Why don't we get going again and see if it's reproducible?"

108

a

109

a

110

A young man hired by a supermarket reported for his first day of work. The manager greeted him with a warm handshake and a smile, gave him a broom and said, "Your first job will be to sweep out the store." "But I'm a college graduate," the young man replied indignantly. "Oh, I'm sorry. I didn't know that," said the manager. "Here, give me the broom – I'll show you how."

111

At the top-secret army headquarters, two generals were testing the new speaking computer. They asked the computer a question: "How long is a piece of string?" After a few moments the computer replied "five thousand". "Five thousand what?" asked one of the generals. "Five thousand, sir" replied the computer. [When talking to an officer, a subordinate is always supposed to say 'sir' at the end of his/her reply]

112

An airplane lands with great difficulty, stopping just short of an accident. When they arrive at the gate, the captain wipes his brow and says: "Wow, that was the shortest runway I've ever seen!" " "You're not kidding," says his co-pilot, looking out of the window. "But it sure is wide". [The plane was traveling across the runway rather than down the runway]

113

There was an engineer who *had* an exceptional gift for fixing all things mechanical. After serving his company loyally for over 30 years, he happily *retired*. Several years later the company *contacted* him regarding a seemingly impossible problem they *were having* with one of their multi-million dollar machines. They *had tried* everything and everyone else to get the machine fixed, but to no avail.

In desperation, they *called* on the retired engineer who *had solved* so many of their problems in the past. The engineer reluctantly took the challenge. He spent a day studying the huge machine. At the end of the day, he marked a small "x" in chalk on a particular component of the machine and proudly stated, "This is where your problem is". The part *was replaced* and the machine *worked* perfectly again. The company *received* a bill for $50,000 from the engineer for his service. They demanded an itemized accounting of his charges. The engineer responded briefly:

One chalk mark: $1

Knowing where to put it: $49,999

114

A graduate with an MBA goes on vacation to the Australian outback. In his travels he comes across a sheep herder with a huge flock. He stops his car, approaches the shepherd and introduces himself.

Always looking to show off his MBA skills, he bets the shepherd he could determine exactly how many sheep are in the flock. If he is right, the graduate gets one sheep. The shepherd agrees.

The MBA graduate goes back to his car, fires up his GPS, laptop and cell phone. He gets a detailed satellite picture of their exact location, downloads the picture and uses grid technology to count the exact number of sheep.

After only a few minutes the graduate walks up to the shepherd and tells him he has 3,766 sheep. The shepherd confirms the number and the proud graduate loads an animal into his car.

Before the graduate can drive away, the shepherd approaches the car and offers to bet him double or nothing that he could guess the graduate's profession. The graduate agrees. The shepherd tells him that he is a consultant.

The amazed graduate confirms this and asks the shepherd how he knew.

The shepherd replies: "You showed the three tell tale signs of all consultants. First, you showed up here without being asked or invited. Second, I paid you to tell me something I already knew. Last, you know absolutely nothing about my business because you just put my dog in your car."

115

No punch line is missing.

116

a

117

b

118

A doctor and a lawyer are talking at a party. Their conversation is constantly interrupted by people describing their ailments and asking the doctor for free medical advice.

After an hour of this, the exasperated doctor asks the lawyer, "What do you do to stop people from asking you for legal advice when you're out of the office?"

"I give it to them," replies the lawyer, "and then I send them a bill."

The doctor is shocked, but agrees to give it a try. The next day, still feeling slightly guilty, the doctor prepares the bills. When he goes to place them in his mailbox, he finds a bill from the lawyer.

119

A man went to his lawyer and asked him, "My neighbor owes me $500 and he won't pay up. What should I do?"

"Do you have any proof he owes you the money?" asked the lawyer. "Nope," replied the man.

"OK, then write him a letter asking him for the $5,000 he owed you," said the lawyer.

"But it's only $500," replied the man. "Precisely. That's what he will reply and then you'll have your proof!"

120

Lawyer: "I have some good news for you" Client: "What good news? You lost my case, I was convicted of a murder I did not commit and was sentenced to die in the electric chair. Lawyer: "That's all true, but I got the voltage lowered".

Key to Chapter 5

121

Two lawyers walking through the woods spotted a vicious looking bear. The first lawyer immediately opened her briefcase, pulled out a pair of sneakers and started putting them on. The second lawyer looked at her and said, "You're crazy! You'll never be able to outrun that bear!" "I don't have to, I only have to outrun you."

122

A lawyer opens the door of his BMW. Suddenly, a passing car hits the door and it flies away. The lawyer gets so mad – he loves his BMW so much! Soon, the police arrive. The lawyer exclaims: "Officer, look what happened to my BMW!" "Lawyers are so materialistic!" says the officer, "You are worried about your stupid BMW! Didn't you notice you're missing your left arm?" "Oh my god! Where is my Rolex!?"

123

A man calls his lawyer and asks: "How much would you charge me to answer three questions" The lawyer replies: "Four hundred dollars. The man retorts: "That's a bit steep don t you think?" And the lawyer replies: "I suppose so. What's you third question?"

124

Did you hear about the terrorist that hijacked an airplane full of lawyers? He threatened to release one every hour if his demands weren't met.

Glossary for Chapter 5

a bit steep	rather expensive (in relation to cost)
accountant	someone who deals with financial records
ailments	medical conditions
beat/beat/beaten	lose a battle
blind	unable to say
brakes	mechanical device to stop the car moving
broom	brush
career	move very rapidly with no control
chalk	material usually used for writing on a blackboard
challenge	difficult task
charges	the amounts he wanted the company to pay him
charge	request a certain amount of money for a service
charity	non-profit organization set up to help people in need
check (GB: cheque)	a piece of paper with a sum of money written on it that the receiver can reclaim at a bank
committee	group of people with a designated task to resolve
conductor	inspector of tickets
cram into	fit into a small space
cut off	terminate, stop someone from talking
dean	head of a university faculty
docked	attached by a rope to the land
donation	money
double or nothing	a gamble to decide whether a debt should be doubled or canceled
enterprise	business
exasperated	frustrated
failed	didn't work
fires up	start a device
fleet of trawlers	a collection of fishing boats
gas	gasoline, petrol
give it a try	make an attempt

guilty	the opposite of innocent
hiding	trying not to be seen
hijacked	illegally take over an aircraft or other vehicle via force
income	money received through work or investment
itemized accounting	a list of all the things he had done plus the relevant costs
lack	absence
limousine	long luxurious car
lose a case	when a lawyer's client is found to be guilty
loyally	without ever changing company
mad	angry
middleman	intermediary
mull over	think about, reflect on
mumble	say unclearly
on a roll	experiencing a prolonged period of success
outrun	run faster than
owes	to be in debt with someone
pen knife	small knife for multiple uses
penniless	with no money
penny	cent (very small amount of money)
perplexed	confused
proof	demonstration
reluctantly	without really wanting to
restroom	bathroom
retire	stop working because you reach a certain age
rod	a mechanical part of the engine
runway	the strip of land at an airport where the planes land
sample size	the number of individual pieces of data collected in a survey
seemingly	apparently
sentence	assign someone a punishment
shepherd/sheep herder	someone who looks after sheep
show up	arrive unexpectedly

sneakers	shoes
spark	spark(ing) plug = device for firing the explosive mixture in an engine
sputter	make a series of soft explosive sounds
steep	going down (up) sharply
string	twisted cotton or other material for tying things with
sweep	the action of cleaning using a brush
to no avail	without success
unharmed	with no injuries
veteran	someone who has fought in a war
wastebasket	recipient for trash
wealthy	rich
wipe his brow	remove the sweat from the top half of his face

Chapter 6
Men and Women

The following three jokes (125, 126 and 127) are all about a common affliction for elderly people - losing their memory. Match the punch lines (a-f) to their related joke. Note: There are six punch lines, but only three jokes.

   a) "Rose, what's the name of that restaurant we went to last night?"
   b) "Why am I knocking on wood?"
   c) "Where's my ice-cream with a cherry on top?"
   d) "Who's Rose?"
   e) "Who's there?"
   f) "Where's the toast?"

125

There was an elderly couple who in their old age noticed that they were getting a lot more forgetful, so they decided to go to the doctor. The doctor told them that they should start writing things down so they don't forget.

They went home and the old lady told her husband to get her a bowl of ice cream. "You might want to write it down," she said.

The husband said, "No, I can remember that you want a bowl of ice cream."

She then told her husband she wanted a bowl of ice cream with whipped cream. "Write it down," she told him

Again he said, "No, no, I can remember: you want a bowl of ice cream with whipped cream."

Then the old lady said she wants a bowl of ice cream with whipped cream and a cherry on top. "Write it down," she told her husband

Again he said, "No, I got it. You want a bowl of ice cream with whipped cream and a cherry on top."

So he goes to get the ice cream and spends an unusually long time in the kitchen, over 30 minutes. He comes out to his wife and hands her a plate of eggs and bacon.

The old wife stares at the plate for a moment, then looks at her husband and asks: "_____"

[forgetful - unable to remember; stares - looks with eyes fixed]

126

An older couple are having dinner at another older couple's home and, after eating, the wives start cleaning up in the kitchen. The two men continue talking about food.

"Last night we went out to that a new Italian restaurant and it turned out to be great," remarks the host. "I recommend it highly if you like pasta."

"What's the place's name?" asks the guest.

The host thinks a bit and asks, "What's the name of that flower you give to someone you love? You know, the one that's red and has thorns."

"Do you mean a rose?"

"That's the one," says the host as he turns toward the kitchen to yell: "_____"

[turn out - reveal itself; yell - shout]

127

Three old ladies are sitting in a cafe chatting about various things.

"You know," says one lady, "I'm getting really forgetful. This morning I was standing at the top of the stairs, and I couldn't remember whether I was going to bed or had just woken up!"

"You think that's bad?" says the second lady. "The other day I was sitting on the edge of my bed, and I couldn't remember whether I was going to bed or had just woken up!"

The third lady smiles smugly.

"Well my memory is just as good as it's always been ... touch wood" she says and knocks the table. Then with a startled look on her face she says: "_____"

[edge - side; smugly - showing excessive satisfaction with oneself; touch wood - phrase said by superstitious people; startled - surprised]

Choose the best explanation (a, b, or c) for joke 128.
- a) The other nine children were from a different father/different fathers.
- b) The wife had just been joking with her husband - in fact he is the father to all ten children, even though one of the them looks different from the others.
- c) The husband is playing a joke on his wife and already knows that he is the father.

128

A very elderly couple is having an elegant dinner to celebrate their 75th wedding anniversary.

The old man leans forward and says softly to his wife, "Dear, there is something that I must ask you. It has always bothered me that our tenth child never quite looked like the rest of our children. Now I want to assure you that these 75 years have been the most wonderful experience I could have ever hoped for, and your answer cannot take that all that away. But, I must know, did he have a different father?"

The wife drops her head, unable to look her husband in the eye, she paused for a moment and then confessed. "Yes. Yes he did."

The old man is very shaken, the reality of what his wife was admitting hit him harder than he had expected. With a tear in his eye he asks "Who? Who was he? Who was the father?"

Again the old woman drops her head, saying nothing at first as she tried to muster the courage to tell the truth to her husband.

Then, finally, she says, "You."

[shaken - emotionally shocked; tear - what your eyes produces when you are sad; muster - find]

The six paragraphs in joke 129 are in the wrong order. Put them in the right order.

129

Personally, we didn't care. We came into town by bus.

So my wife called him an idiot. He finished the second ticket and put it on the windshield with the first. Then he started writing a third ticket. This went on for about 20 minutes. The more we abused him, the more tickets he wrote.

We try to have a little fun each day now that we're retired. It's important at our age.

We went up to him and said, 'Come on man, how about giving a senior citizen a break?' He ignored us and continued writing the ticket. I called him a fascist pig. He glared at me and started writing another ticket for having worn tires.

Well, for example, the other day my wife and I went to our local shopping center and went into a shop. We were only in there for about 5 minutes. When we came out there was a traffic warden writing out a parking ticket.

Working people frequently ask retired people what they do to make their days interesting.

> [not care - not worried or concerned; ticket - parking fine (i.e. money to be paid to local administration for parking illegally); windshield - glass at the front of a car; retired - no longer working because have reached the age of retirement (typically 60-65); give someone a break - leave someone alone; call someone a fascist pig - strong insult; glare - look at someone angrily; traffic warden - someone employed to make sure citizens park in the right place]

Below are five explanations (a-e) for the two jokes below (130, 131). Match an appropriate explanation with each joke.

   a) *The doctor realizes that the old man's medical condition has not improved at all.*
   b) *The old man can how understand how his family really feel about him.*
   c) *The old man feels fresh and full of life like a young child.*
   d) *The old man thinks he is at home rather than at the hospital.*
   e) *The old man thought he was a patient, whereas he was just a visitor.*

130

An elderly man goes to the doctor to be fitted with badly-needed hearing aids. A month later he goes back for a checkup. Both he and the doctor are enthused with his increased hearing.

"Your family must really be pleased that you can hear so well again," the doctor says.

"Oh, I haven't told any of them yet. I just sit around and listen to the conversations. So far I've changed my will three times."

[fitted with - fix in place; hearing aid - device to enable the wearer to hear better; enthused - very happy and satisfied; will - a legal document specifying how you wish your money and property to be dealt with when you die]

131

Hospital regulations require a wheelchair for patients being discharged. However, one older gentleman - already dressed and sitting on a bed with a suitcase at his feet - insists to the doctor that he doesn't need her help to leave the hospital. But she insists, so he reluctantly lets her wheel him into the elevator.

On the way down the doctor asks him if his wife is meeting him.

"I don't know now," he replies. "She's still upstairs in the bathroom changing out of her hospital gown."

[discharge - be officially allowed to leave a hospital after being a patient there; wheel - push him on the wheelchair; reluctantly - against his wishes; gown - dress]

For the jokes in 132, match the questions with the answers (a-l).

132

Questions

How are husbands like lawn mowers?
How can you tell if a man is lying?
How can you tell if your man is happy?
How do males exercise on the beach?
How do men define a "50/50" relationship?
How do you get a man to stop biting his nails?
How do you scare a man?
How does a man show he's planning for the future?
How is a man like a used car?
How long does it take a man to change the toilet paper?
How many men does it take to open a beer?
How many men does it take to screw in a light bulb?

Answers

a) Both are easy to get, cheap, and unreliable!
b) By sucking in their stomachs every time they see a bikini
c) He buys two cases of beer instead of one.
d) Make him wear shoes.
e) None. It should be opened by the time she brings it to the couch.
f) One. He just holds it up there and waits for the world to revolve around him.
g) Sneak up behind him and start throwing rice!
h) They're hard to get started, they emit noxious odors, and half the time they don't work.
i) We cook-they eat; we clean-they dirty; we iron-they wrinkle.
j) We don't know it's never happened.
k) Who cares?
l) You can see his lips moving.

[lawnmower - machine for cutting the grass; lying - not telling the truth; bite his nails - eat the ends of his fingers; scare - make afraid; sucking in - breathing in so that stomach appears to be flatter; couch - sofa; sneak up - walk up behind someone quietly; noxious odors - horrible, polluting smells; wrinkle - to make unwanted lines and folds in clothes; lips - external part of mouth]

For jokes 133 and 134, choose the correct tense.

133

The CEO of Microsoft is deep in conversation with the chairman of General Motors.

"If automotive technology *had kept/would have kept* pace with computer technology over the past few decades," boasts Microsoft's CEO, "you *would now be/would have now been* driving a V-32 instead of a V-8, and it *would have/would have had* a top speed of 10,000 miles per hour. Or, you *could have/could have had* an economy car that weighs 30 pounds and gets a thousand miles to a gallon of gas. In either case, the cost of a new car *would/would have been* less than $50."

"Sure," says the General Motors chairman. "But *will/would* you really want to drive a car that crashes four times a day?"

> [keep pace with - be in line with; boast - talk with excessive self-satisfaction; top speed - maximum speed; 30 pounds = 13.6 kg; gallon = 3.8 liters]

134

A New York businessman boarded a train in Albany on his way to Buffalo. As it was a night train, he took a sleeper car and gave the porter strict instructions to waken him and put him off in Buffalo.

"I'm a very heavy sleeper," the passenger said, "and I *can/may/would* give you a hard time. But whatever you do, make sure to put me off in Buffalo... even if you *have/will have/would have* to put me off in my pajamas."

The next morning, the man woke up to find himself in Cleveland. He located the porter and abused him verbally.

After the man left, a bystander asked the porter how he *could* stand there and take that verbal abuse.

"That wasn't anything," the porter replied. "You *should've heard/will have heard/would have heard* the guy I put off in Buffalo.

> [boarded - got on; sleeper car - train wagon where you can sleep; give someone a hard time - make things difficult for someone; put me off - let me get off the train; bystander - someone who happened to be there at the time]

Insert the following phrases into the correct position in joke 135.

a) Hey, you just went through a red light.
b) Don't worry about it. My brother does it all the time
c) Hey man, you just went through another red light. What the heck are you doing?
d) What the heck? You're going to get us killed! Pull over and let me out."
e) I'm telling you: don't worry about it.
f) You go flying past three red lights, almost getting us killed, and then you slam on the brakes when you have a green light?
g) I had to stop; my brother might have been coming

135

Two guys are driving down 5th Avenue in Manhattan when they come up to a red light. The guy driving slams the gas pedal and they go zooming past the red light.

His friend looks at him and says, "_____."

The guy driving says, ""_____."

So they keep driving and they come to a second red light. The guy driving slams on the gas pedal and zooms past another red light. His friend is pretty mad, looks at him and says,

"_____"

The guy driving tells his friend, "Don't worry about it. My brother does this all the time."

They come to a third red light and the guy driving slams on the gas, zooming past the red light. His friend starts screaming at him,

"_____."

The guy driving screams back at him, "My brother, he does it all the time."

So they keep driving and they come to a green light. The guy driving slams on the brakes.

His friend looks at him and says, "Are you out of your mind? What is wrong with you? "_____?"

The guy driving looks at his friend and says, "_____"

> [red light - traffic light; what the heck - exclamation of surprise; slam the gas pedal - put his foot down hard on the accelerator; zoom - go very fast; pretty mad - quite angry; out of your mind - crazy]

For each of the following jokes (136-139) decide the best punch line (a, b, or c).

136

Passengers on a plane are waiting for the flight to leave. The entrance door opens at the back of the plane, and two men walk up the aisle, dressed in pilot uniforms. Both are wearing dark glasses. One has a dog for the blind, and the other is tapping his way up the aisle with a cane. Nervous laughter spreads through the cabin, but the men enter the cockpit, the door closes, and the engines start. The passengers begin glancing nervously, searching for some sign that this is just a little practical joke. None is forthcoming. The plane moves faster and faster down the runway, and people at the windows realize that they're headed straight for the water at the edge of the airport. As it begins to look as though the plane will never take off, that it will plow into the water, screams of panic fill the cabin. But at that moment, the plane lifts smoothly into the air. Up in the cockpit, the co-pilot turns to the pilot and says:

- a) "You know, Jack, one of these days, they're going to scream too late, and we're all going to die."
- b) "I hope no one realizes that we are both totally blind."
- c) "Thank goodness we were on automatic pilot."

[aisle - corridor; tapping with a cane - using the white stick that the blind (people who can't see) use; cockpit - where the pilots sit; glancing - looking around; practical joke - trick; take off - go into the air; plow (GB: plough) - crash into; smoothly - without difficulty; be on automatic pilot - when the plane flies itself without the intervention of a human pilot]

137

It was her first trip to Hawaii and the middle aged lady had noticed that several of her fellow passengers did not pronounce the island name as she had previously assumed it should be pronounced. Anxious not to offend the natives of the island, she decided to approach the first islander she saw and said: "Excuse me, sir, I wonder if you could tell me if it is pronounced Hawaii or Havaii?"

"Havaii," the man responded.

"Thank you very much," said the grateful tourist.

- a) "You bet!" said the man.
- b) "You're velcome!" said the man.
- c) "You're welcome!" said the man.

[You bet - You're welcome]

138

An old guy in his car is driving home from work when his wife rings him on his car phone.

"Honey", she says in a worried voice, "be careful. There was a bit on the news just now, some lunatic is driving the wrong way down the freeway".

- a) "It's worse than that", he replies, "there are hundreds of them!"
- b) "Don't worry," he replies. "I decided to take an alternative route."
- c) "Yes, I know, he's going to cause any accident any minute now … aaaaahhhh!"

[honey - term of affection; lunatic - crazy person; wrong way - opposite to the correct direction; freeway - main road with several lanes]

139

A large two-engine train was crossing America. After the train had gone some distance one of the engines broke down.

"No problem," the engineer thought, and carried on at half-power.

Further on down the line, the other engine broke down, and the train came to a standstill.

The engineer decided he should inform the passengers about why the train had stopped, and made the following announcement:

"Ladies and gentlemen, I have some good news and some bad news. The bad news is that both engines have failed, and we will be stuck here for some time. The good news is that …

- a) at least we haven't derailed.
- b) the signal is on red. We would have had to stop in any case.
- c) this is a train and not a plane.

[break down - cease to function, fail; come to a standstill - stop moving; be stuck - be immobile]

Choose the punch line (a, b or c) for this very long but fun joke (140).

    a) "Sorry," he replied, "but can I ask if you have any protection?"
    b) "Sorry darling, but I've got a headache."
    c) "You mean …" he replied, "I can check my e-mail from here?"

140

A hurricane came unexpectedly. The ship went down and was lost. The man found himself swept up on the shore of an island with no other people, no supplies, nothing. Only bananas and coconuts. Used to 5-star hotels, this guy had no idea what to do, so for the next four months he ate bananas, drank coconut juice and fixed his gaze on the sea, hoping to spot a rescue ship.

One day, as he was lying on the beach, he spotted movement out of the corner of his eye. It was a rowboat, and in it was the most gorgeous woman he had ever seen.

She rowed up to him. In disbelief, he asked her: "Where did you come from? How did you get here?"

"I rowed from the other side of the island," she said. "I landed here when my cruise ship sank."

"Amazing," he said. "I didn't know anyone else had survived. How many are there? You were lucky to have a rowboat wash up with you."

"It's only me," she said, "and the rowboat didn't wash up; nothing did."

He was confused. "Then how did you get the rowboat?"

"Oh, simple," replied the woman. "I made the rowboat out of materials that I found on the island. The oars were made from Gum tree branches. I wove the bottom from palm branches and the sides and stern came from a Eucalyptus tree."

"B-B-But that's impossible," stuttered the man. "You had no tools or hardware. How did you manage?"

"Oh, that was no problem," replied the woman. "On the other side of the island there is a very unusual stratum of alluvial rock exposed. I found that if I fired it to a certain temperature in my kiln, it melted into forgeable ductile iron. I used that for tools, and used the tools to make the hardware. But enough of that," she said. "Where do you live?"

Sheepishly, he confessed that he had been sleeping on the beach the whole time.

"Well, let's row over to my place, then," she said.

After a few minutes of rowing she docked the boat at a small wharf. As the man looked to the shore he nearly fell out of the boat. Before him was a stone walk leading to an exquisite bungalow painted in blue and white. While the woman tied up the rowboat, the man could only stare ahead, dumbstruck.

As they walked into the house, she said casually, "It's not much, but I call it home. Sit down, please; would you like a drink?"

"No, no thank you," he said, still dazed. "I can't take any more coconut juice."

"It's not coconut juice," the woman replied. "I have been making my own alcohol. How about a Pina Colada?"

Trying to hide his amazement, the man accepted, and they sat down on her couch to talk.

After they had exchanged their stories, the woman announced, "I'm going to slip into something comfortable. Would you like to take a shower and shave? There is a razor upstairs in the cabinet in the bathroom."

No longer questioning anything, the man went into the bathroom. There in the cabinet was a razor made from a bone handle.

"This woman is amazing," he mused. "What next?"

When he returned, she greeted him wearing nothing but vines - strategically positioned. She beckoned for him to sit down next to her.

"Tell me," she began, "we've been out here for a very long time. You've been lonely. There's something I'm sure you really feel like doing right now, something you've been longing for all these months. You know…"

She stared into his eyes. He couldn't believe what he was hearing.

[used to - accustomed to; fixed his gaze - looked carefully; rescue ship - a ship that would find him; rowboat - small boat powered by oars (pole with a flat side); gorgeous - very beautiful; survived - not killed; wash up - appear from the sea; wove - made; stern - back of boat; tools - utensils; fired - heated; kiln - furnace; sheepishly - rather embarrassed; row - transport oneself in a rowboat; wharf - landing place; dumbstruck - unable to speak, in a state of shock; couch - sofa; slip into - change clothes; razor - device for shaving, removing hair from face; beckoned - made a movement with hand to indicate that he should come near her; long for - really want; stared - looked with fixed eyes]

For the jokes in 141, match the questions with the answers (a-j).

141

Questions

1. What are a married man's two greatest assets?
2. What did God say after creating man?
3. What do men and mascara have in common?
4. What do most men consider a gourmet restaurant?
5. What do you call a group of men waiting for a haircut?
6. What do you call a man that lost all of his intelligence?
7. What do you call a man with an opinion?
8. What do you call a man with half a brain?
9. What do you call a married man vacuuming?
10. What has eight arms and an IQ of 60?

Answers

a. A barbecue.
b. A closed mouth and an open wallet.
c. A widow.
d. Any place without a drive-up window.
e. Doing what he's told.
f. Four guys watching a football game.
g. Gifted.
h. I can do so much better.
i. They both run at the first sign of emotion.
j. Wrong.

[assets - possessions; mascara - black line for eyes; vacuuming - cleaning using an electric device; barbecue - cooking device for use outdoors; drive-up window - place where you can buy fast food directly from your car; gifted - talented]

For joke 142, insert man/men *or* woman/women *into the spaces.*

142

Why are married _____ heavier than single _____? Single _____ come home, see what's in the fridge and go to bed. Married _____ come home, see what's in bed and go to the fridge.

Why did God create _____ before _____? Because you're always supposed to have a rough draft before creating your masterpiece.

Why did God create _____ before _____? He didn't want any advice

Why do _____ like smart _____? Opposites attract.

Why do _____ need instant replay on TV sports? Because after 30 seconds they forget what happened.

Why do so few _____ end up in heaven? They never stop to ask directions

Why don't some _____ have a mid-life crisis? They're stuck in adolescence.

Why is it difficult to find _____ who are sensitive, caring and good-looking? They already have boyfriends.

Why is psychoanalysis a lot quicker for _____ than for _____? When it's time to go back to his childhood, he's already there.

Why do little boys whine? Because they're practising to be _____.

[rough draft - first version; masterpiece - best work; heaven - place where dead people go if they have lived a good life; whine - cry and complain]

Key to Chapter 6

125

"Where's the toast?"

126

"Rose, what's the name of that restaurant we went to last night?"

127

"Who's there?"

128

a

129

Working people frequently ask retired people what they do to make their days interesting.

Well, for example, the other day my wife and I went to Taunton and went into a shop. We were only in there for about 5 minutes. When we came out there was a traffic warden writing out a parking ticket.

We went up to him and said, 'Come on man, how about giving a senior citizen a break?' He ignored us and continued writing the ticket. I called him a fascist pig. He glared at me and started writing another ticket for having worn tires.

So my wife called him an idiot. He finished the second ticket and put it on the windshield with the first. Then he started writing a third ticket. This went on for about 20 minutes. The more we abused him, the more tickets he wrote.

Personally, we didn't care. We came into town by bus.

We try to have a little fun each day now that we're retired. It's important at our age.

130

b

131

e

132

How are husbands like lawn mowers? They're hard to get started, they emit noxious odors, and half the time they don't work.

How can you tell if a man is lying? You can see his lips moving.

How can you tell if your man is happy? Who cares?

How do males exercise on the beach? By sucking in their stomachs every time they see a bikini.

How do men define a "50/50" relationship? We cook-they eat; we clean-they dirty; we iron-they wrinkle.

How do you get a man to stop biting his nails? Make him wear shoes.

How do you scare a man? Sneak up behind him and start throwing rice!

How does a man show he's planning for the future? He buys two cases of beer instead of one.

How is a man like a used car? Both are easy to get, cheap, and unreliable!

How long does it take a man to change the toilet paper? We don't know it's never happened.

How many men does it take to open a beer? None. It should be opened by the time she brings it to the couch.

How many men does it take to screw in a light bulb? One. He just holds it up there and waits for the world to revolve around him.

133

The CEO of Microsoft is deep in conversation with the chairman of General Motors. "If automotive technology *had kept* pace with computer technology over the past few decades," boasts Microsoft's CEO, "you *would now be* driving a V-32 instead of a V-8, and it *would have* a top speed of 10,000 miles per hour. Or, you *could have* an economy car that weighs 30 pounds and gets a thousand miles to a gallon of gas. In either case, the cost of a new car *would be* less than $50." "Sure," says the General Motors chairman. "But *would* you really want to drive a car that crashes four times a day?"

134

A New York businessman boarded a train in Albany on his way to Buffalo. As it was a night train, he took a sleeper car and gave the porter strict instructions to waken him and put him off in Buffalo. "I'm a very heavy sleeper," the passenger said, "and I *may* give you a hard time. But whatever you do, make sure to put me off in Buffalo… even if you *have* to put me off in my pajamas." The next morning, the man woke up to find himself in Cleveland. He located the porter and abused him verbally. After the man left, a bystander asked the porter how he *could* stand there and take that verbal abuse. "That wasn't anything," the porter replied. "You *should've heard* the guy I put off in Buffalo.

135

Two guys are driving down 5th Avenue in Manhattan when they come up to a red light. The guy driving slams the gas pedal and they go zooming past the red light.

His friend looks at him and says, "*Hey, you just went through a red light.*"

The guy driving says, "*Don't worry about it. My brother does it all the time.*"

So they keep driving and they come to a second red light. The guy driving slams on the gas pedal and zooms past another red light. His friend is pretty mad, looks at him and says,

"*Hey man, you just went through another red light. What the heck are you doing?*"

The guy driving tells his friend, "Don't worry about it. My brother does this all the time."

They come to a third red light and the guy driving slams on the gas, zooming past the red light. His friend starts screaming at him,

"*What the heck? You're going to get us killed! Pull over and let me out.*"

The guy driving screams back at him, "*I'm telling you: don't worry about it. My brother, he does it all the time.*"

So they keep driving and they come to a green light. The guy driving slams on the brakes.

His friend looks at him and says, "Are you out of your mind? What the heck is wrong with you? *You go flying past three red lights, almost getting us killed, and then you slam on the brakes when you have a green light?*"

The guy driving looks at his friend and says, "*I had to stop; my brother might have been coming.*"

136

a

137

b

138

a

139

c

140

c

141

1. What are a married man's two greatest assets? A closed mouth and an open wallet.

2. What did God say after creating man? I can do so much better.

3. What do men and mascara have in common? They both run at the first sign of emotion.

4. What do most men consider a gourmet restaurant? Any place without a drive-up window.

5. What do you call a group of men waiting for a haircut? A barbecue.

6. What do you call a man that lost all of his intelligence? A widow.

7. What do you call a man with an opinion? Wrong.

8. What do you call a man with half a brain? Gifted.

9. What do you call a married man vacuuming? Doing what he's told..

10. What has eight arms and an IQ of 60? Four guys watching a football game.

142

Why are married women heavier than single women? Single women come home, see what's in the fridge and go to bed. Married women come home, see what's in bed and go to the fridge.

Why did God create man before woman? Because you're always supposed to have a rough draft before creating your masterpiece

Why did God create man before woman? He didn't want any advice

Why do men like smart women? Opposites attract.

Why do men need instant replay on TV sports? Because after 30 seconds they forget what happened.

Why do so few men end up in Heaven? They never stop to ask directions

Why don't some men have a mid-life crisis? They're stuck in adolescence.

Why is it difficult to find men who are sensitive, caring and good-looking? They already have boyfriends.

Why is psychoanalysis a lot quicker for men than for women? When it's time to go back to his childhood, he's already there.

Why do little boys whine? Because they're practising to be men.

Glossary for Chapter 6

aisle	corridor
assets	possessions
barbecue	cooking device for use outdoors
be on automatic pilot	when the plane flies itself without the intervention of a human pilot
be stuck	be immobile
beckoned	made a movement with hand to indicate that he should come near her
bite one's nails	eat the ends of one's fingers
board	get on (plane, train, bus)
boast	talk with excessive self-satisfaction
break down	cease to function, fail
bystander	someone who happened to be there at the time
cockpit	where the pilots sit
come to a standstill	stop moving
couch	sofa
couch	sofa
discharge	be officially allowed to leave a hospital after being a patient there
drive-up window	place where you can buy fast food directly from your car
dumbstruck	unable to speak, in a state of shock
edge	side
enthused	very happy and satisfied
fired	heated
fitted with	equipped with
fix one's gaze	look carefully
forgetful	prone to not being able to remember
freeway	main road with several lanes
gifted	talented
give someone a break	leave someone alone
give someone a hard time	make things difficult for someone
glancing	looking around
glare	look at someone angrily
gorgeous	very beautiful

gown	dress
hearing aid	device to enable the wearer to hear better
heaven	place where dead people go if they have lived a good life
honey	term of affection
keep pace with	be in line with
kiln	furnace
lawnmower	machine for cutting the grass
lips	external part of mouth
long for	really want
lunatic	crazy person
lying	not telling the truth
mascara	black line for eyes
masterpiece	best work
muster	find
not care	not worried or concerned
noxious odors	horrible, polluting smells
out of your mind	crazy
plow (GB: plough)	crash into
practical joke	trick
pretty mad	quite angry
razor	device for shaving, removing hair from face
red light	traffic light
reluctantly	against his wishes
rescue ship	a ship that would find him
retired	no longer working because have reached the age of retirement (typically 60-65)
rough draft	first version
row	transport oneself in a rowboat
rowboat	small boat powered by oars (pole with a flat side)
scare	make afraid
shaken	emotionally shocked
sheepishly	rather embarrassed
slam the gas pedal	put his foot down hard on the accelerator
sleeper car	train wagon where you can sleep
slip into	change into very casual clothes

smoothly	without difficulty
smugly	showing excessive satisfaction with oneself
sneak up	walk up behind someone quietly
stare	look with fixed eyes
startled	surprised
stern	back of boat
survive	not be killed
take off	go into the air
tapping with a cane	using the white stick that the blind (people who can't see) use
tear	what your eyes produces when you are sad
ticket	parking fine (i.e. money to be paid to local administration for parking illegally)
tools	utensils
top speed	maximum speed
touch wood	phrase said by superstitious people
traffic warden	someone employed to make sure citizens park in the right place
turn out	reveal itself
used to	accustomed to
vacuuming	cleaning using an electric device
wash up	appear from the sea
wharf	landing place
what the heck	exclamation of surprise
wheel	push him on the wheelchair
whine	cry and complain
will	a legal document specifying how you wish your money and property to be dealt with when you die
windshield	glass at the front of a car
wove	made
wrinkle	to make unwanted lines and folds in clothes
wrong way	opposite to the correct direction
yell	shout
You bet	You're welcome
zoom	go very fast

Chapter 7
School

Match the beginnings of these jokes (143) with their endings.

143

Beginnings

Teacher: What did Shakespeare use to write with?
Teacher: I'm afraid your son has swallowed a coin.
Father: What position are you playing in the school football team?
Teacher: Tell me two pronouns?
Teacher: I hope I didn't see you looking at Rachel's paper.
Pupil: I don't think I deserve a zero on this test.

Endings

a) Mother: That's alright it was his lunch money.
b) Pupil: A pencil - either a 2B or not 2B.
c) Pupil: I hope you didn't either.
d) Pupil: Who? Me?
e) Son: The coach says I am the main drawback.
f) Teacher: I agree, but it's the lowest mark I can give you.

[swallowed a coin - now has a piece of metal money in his stomach; paper - sheet of paper with answers given by a student in a written test; deserve - merit; coach - sports trainer; mark - score]

The following jokes (144-148) are about Johnny (a generic male child who often misbehaves or is impolite), his teacher and his dad.

Match the punch lines (a-e) with the jokes.

   a) A jack.
   b) It wasn't one person, Miss. My dad helped me.
   c) No, he did it all.
   d) So I decided to wait until it settles down.
   e) You don't know my daddy.

> [jack - the card that comes between a ten and a queen in a pack of cards; dad, daddy - father; settle down - stop changing]

144

"If you had a dollar," quizzed the teacher, "and you asked your father for another dollar and fifty cents, how much money would you have?"

"One dollar," answered little Johnny.

"You don't know your basic math," said the teacher shaking her head, disappointed.

Little Johnny shook his head too: "_____."

145

"It's clear" said the teacher, "That you haven't studied your geography. What's your excuse?"

"Well, my dad says the world is changing every day. _____."

146

The teacher asks little Johnny if he knows his numbers.

"Yes," he says. "My daddy taught me."

"Can you tell me what comes after three?"

"Four," answers little Johnny.

"What comes after six?"

"Seven," answers little Johnny.

"Very good," says the teacher. "Your father did a very fine job. What comes after ten?"

"_____" answers little Johnny.

147

Teacher: Johnny, did you father help you with your homework last night?

Johnny: "_____."

148

Teacher: "Johnny, your homework is very poor. I really don't see how one person can make so many mistakes."

Johnny: "_____."

For each joke (149-152) choose the best punch line (a, b, or c).

149

In class one day, Mr. Johnson summoned Johnny over to his desk after a test, and said:

"Johnny I have a feeling that you have been cheating on your tests."

Johnny was astounded and asked Mr. Johnson to prove it.

"Well", said Mr. Johnson, "I was looking over your test and the question was, 'Who was our first president?', and the little girl that sits next to you, Mary, put 'George Washington,' and so did you."

"So what? Everyone knows that he was the first president."

"Well, just wait a minute," said Mr. Johnson. "The next question was, 'Who freed the slaves?' Mary put Abraham Lincoln and so did you."

"Well, I read the history book last night and I remembered that," said Johnny.

"Wait, wait," said Mr. Johnson. "The next question was, 'Who was president during the Louisiana Purchase?' Mary put 'I don't know,' and you put _____ ."

   a) Nor do I.
   b) Donald Trump.
   c) Mickey Mouse.

[summoned - ask officially to come; cheating - copying from another person; astounded - very surprised; freed the slaves - liberated the non-free citizens]

150

When little Johnny was in the fifth grade he looked downcast, so her teacher asked, "What's the problem, Johnny, I hope it's not homework again"?

"Well, yes it is", replied Johnny. "I was stupid and made my homework paper into a paper airplane".

"Johnny, you're right that wasn't a very bright thing to do", said the teacher, "but this once I'll let you just unfold the paper and hand it in".

"Oh, but that won't work", said Johnny, looking even sadder. "You see, _____".

- a) the plane was hijacked.
- b) I left it at home.
- c) I threw it out of the window.

[fifth grade - 10-11 year olds; downcast - unhappy; bright - intelligent; this once - just for this occasion; unfold the paper - make the paper flat again; hand it in - consign; hijacked - taken over by terrorists]

151

Mother: How was school today, Johnny?

Johnny: It was really great mum! Today we made explosives!

Mother: They do very fancy stuff with you these days. And what will you do at school tomorrow?

Johnny: _____

- a) We're going to rob a bank.
- b) What school?
- c) We're going to learn how to make a bomb.

[fancy stuff - sophisticated, interesting things]

152

Teacher: "If you think you are stupid, I want you to stand up."

Nobody stands up. Teacher: "I'm sure there are some stupid students over here!!"

Johnny stands up. Teacher: "Oh, Johnny, you think you're stupid?"

Johnny: _____

    a) "I don't think it. I know it. You told me so."
    b) "No. I just feel bad that you're standing alone."
    c) "No, I just needed some exercise."

Insert the following sentences into the appropriate joke (153-159).

    a) All right… "I am the ninth letter of the alphabet."
    b) Here it is!
    c) No, but the kid who sits next to me was.
    d) Of course not.
    e) Thank goodness!
    f) That's impossible
    g) Why are you late?

153

Teacher: How old were you on your last birthday?

Pupil: Seven.

Teacher: How old will you be on your next birthday?

Pupil: Nine.

Teacher: _____ .

Pupil: No, it isn't, Teacher. I'm eight today.

154

Boy: Isn't the principal a dummy!

Girl: Do you know who I am?

Boy: No.

Girl: I'm the principal's daughter.

Boy: And do you know who I am?

Girl: No.

Boy: _____ .

[principal - head of school]

155

Teacher: George, go to the map and find North America.

Pupil: _____ .

Teacher: Correct. Now, class, who discovered America?

Class: George!

156

Pupil: Teacher, would you punish me for something I didn't do?

Teacher: _____ .

Pupil: Good, because I didn't do my homework.

157

Teacher: _____ .

Pupil: Because of the sign.

Teacher: What sign?

Pupil: The one that says, "School Ahead, Go Slow."

[School Ahead, Go Slow - a road sign warning motorists that there is a school nearby and that they should drive slowly]

158

Mother: Why did you get such a low mark on that test?

Son: Because of absence.

Mother: You mean you were absent on the day of the test?

Son: _____ .

159

Teacher: Ellen, give me a sentence starting with "I".

Pupil: I is…

Teacher: No, Ellen. Always say, "I am."

Pupil: _____ .

Insert the names of the people (a-f) into the jokes (160-164) into the right places.

   a) *Class comedian*
   b) *Father/mother*
   c) *Hygiene teacher*
   d) *Mother/father*
   e) *Pupil*
   f) *Son*

160

Mother: Why on earth did you swallow the money I gave you?

_____ : You said it was my lunch money.

> [swallow - allow food or drink to go down one's throat and into one's stomach]

161

Teacher: If you received $10 from 10 people, what would you get?

_____ : A new bike.

> [get - *obtain a result* in math, *buy* when you receive money from a person]

162

Teacher: If I had seven oranges in one hand and eight oranges in the other, what would I have?

_____ : Big hands!

163

_____ : How can you prevent diseases caused by biting insects?

Pupil: Don't bite any.

> [prevent - avoid, by biting insects - ambiguous sentence: if you bite insects deliberately or if insects bite you]

164

Teacher: Well, at least there's one thing I can say about your son.

_____ : What's that?

Teacher: With grades like these, he couldn't be cheating.

[grade - score, cheat - copy from another person during a test]

165

Daughter: Dad, can you write in the dark?

_____ : I think so. What do you want me to write?

Daughter: Your name on this report card.

[report card - card showing a pupil's results in all the subjects. Generally this card has to be shown to the parents who then have to sign it to prove that they have read it]

Below are eight paragraphs from two jokes (166 and 167) that have been mixed up. Each joke has four paragraphs. See if you can recreate the two jokes.

Joke 166 (professor who is a generous marker): ____ ____ ____ ____

Joke 167 (picnic): ____ ____ ____ ____

166 and 167

1) A professor was known for being a generous marker. The grades he gave for one of his courses were based solely on two exams and the stuff on the exams was covered entirely in the textbook. As word of the course spread each term there was a large group of students who turned up infrequently, or not at all - just showing up for the exams.
2) "Circle the picture of the professor who teaches this course."
3) (For 95 points): Which tire?
4) Finally, it got so bad that one term about half of the students never turned up at all until the exams. On the day of first exam, the students sat down and a graduate assistant handed out the papers. The assistant explained: "The professor is ill, so I'll be taking the exams."
5) Five students were so confident that the weekend before their final exams, they decided to go for a picnic and party with some friends up there. They had a great time. However, after all the partying, they slept all day Sunday and didn't make it back to College until early Monday morning. Rather than taking the final exam then, they decided to find their professor after the final and explain to him why they had

missed it. They explained that they had gone to an old people's home in the nearest town to spend some time with aged people for the weekend with the plan to come back and study but, unfortunately, they had a flat tire on the way back, didn't have a spare, and couldn't get help for a long time. As a result, they missed the final exam.
6) When the Professor had thought it over he agreed they could make up the final the following day. The students were elated and relieved. They studied that night and went in the next day at the time the professor had told them. He placed them in separate rooms and handed each student a test booklet, and told them to begin.
7) They looked at the first problem, worth 5 points. It was the easiest question in their entire syllabus. "Cool," they thought at the same time, each one in his separate room. "This is going to be easy." Each finished the problem and then turned the page. On the second page was written:
8) When they opened the booklet the students discovered just one question. It listed twenty rather poor quality photos of the academic staff. The instructions read:

[marker - assigning marks/grades to a test; solely - only; turned up - attend; show up - come; tire - rubber that covers the wheel of a car; make it back - manage to return; spare - an extra tire; elated - happy; relieved - not anxious any more]

Joke 168 is about a university student who is taking an important exam. He hasn't studied enough and exceeds the official duration of the exam. But he has a clever plan to save himself ...

Put the sentences into the correct order in order to be able to read the joke.

168

a) "I will absolutely not accept any papers given to me after the two-hour deadline has passed." Two hours later he broke the silence.
b) "No," said the professor.
c) "Terrific," replied the student and stuffed his paper into the middle of the pile of the other examination papers.
d) "Time is up," he said. But one student continued to work furiously.
e) "You will have exactly two hours," said the professor as he handed out examination papers to a roomful of engineering students.
f) Almost 15 minutes later, the student went up to the professor who was sitting behind the pile of examination papers handed in by the other students.
g) When the professor refused to accept the student's paper, the student drew himself up to his full height and asked: "Professor, do you know who I am?"

[stuffed - inserted; pile - lots of papers on top of each other; handed in - consigned; drew himself up to his full height - made himself look as tall as possible]

Jokes 169-175 have no specific exercise. Simply enjoy them! See the key for an explanation of the jokes.

169

Teacher: What is the chemical formula for water?

Johnny: "HIJKLMNO"!!

Teacher: What are you talking about?

Johnny: Yesterday you said it's H to O!

170

While visiting a country school, the chairman of the Board Of Education became provoked at the noise the unruly students were making in the next room. Angrily, he opened the door and grabbed one of the taller boys who seemed to be doing most of the talking. He dragged the boy to the next room and stood him in the corner. A few minutes later, a small boy stuck his head in the room and pleaded, "Please, sir, may we have our teacher back?"

> [Board Of Education - commission responsible for ensuring good standards in schools; unruly - noisy and disorganized; grabbed - took hold of; dragged - pulled; stuck - put; have back - return]

171

Why did the teacher wear dark glasses? Because her class was so bright.

172

Why has the teacher cross-eyes? He couldn't control his pupils.

173

Two young men who had just graduated from university climbed into a taxi wearing their graduation gowns.

"Are you graduates from the city university?" asked the cab driver.

"Yes, sir," they announced proudly. "Class of 2018."

The cabbie extended his hand. "Class of 2008"

174

Little Johnny's kindergarten class was on a field trip to their local police station where they saw pictures, tacked to a bulletin board, of the 10 most wanted criminals. One of the youngsters pointed to a picture and asked if it really was the photo of a wanted person.

"Yes," said the policeman. "The detectives want very badly to capture him."

Little Johnny asked, "Why didn't you keep him when you took his picture?"

[kindergarten - school for very young children; field trip - school trip; tacked - attached; youngster - young person]

175

Teacher: Didn't you promise to behave?

Little Johnny: Yes, sir.

Teacher: And didn't I promise to punish you if you didn't?

Little Johnny: Yes, sir, but since I broke my promise, you didn't have to keep yours.

Key to Chapter 7

143

Teacher: What did Shakespeare use to write with? Pupil: A pencil - either a 2B or not 2B.

Teacher: I'm afraid your son has swallowed a coin. Mother: That's alright it was his lunch money.

Father: What position are you playing in the school football team? Son: The coach says I am the main drawback.

Teacher: Tell me two pronouns? Pupil: Who? Me?

Teacher: I hope I didn't see you looking at Rachel's paper. Pupil: I hope you didn't either.

Pupil: I don't think I deserve a zero on this test. Teacher: I agree, but it's the lowest mark I can give you.

144

"If you had a dollar," quizzed the teacher, "and you asked your father for another dollar and fifty cents, how much money would you have?" "One dollar," answered little Johnny. "You don't know your basic math," said the teacher shaking her head, disappointed. Little Johnny shook his head too: "You don't know my daddy."

145

"It's clear" said the teacher, "That you haven't studied your geography. What's your excuse?" "Well, my dad says the world is changing every day. So I decided to wait until it settles down!"

146

The teacher asks little Johnny if he knows his numbers. "Yes," he says. "My daddy taught me." "Can you tell me what comes after three?" "Four," answers little Johnny. "What comes after six?" "Seven," answers little Johnny. "Very good," says the teacher. "Your father did a very fine job. What comes after ten?" "A jack," answers little Johnny.

147

Johnny, did you father help you with your homework last night? No, he did it all.

148

Teacher: Johnny, your homework is very poor. I really don't see how one person can make so many mistakes. Johnny: It wasn't one person, Miss. My dad helped me.

Key to Chapter 7

149

a

150

a

151

b

152

b

153

Teacher: How old were you on your last birthday? Pupil: Seven. Teacher: How old will you be on your next birthday? Pupil: Nine. Teacher: That's impossible. Pupil: No, it isn't, Teacher. I'm eight today.

154

Boy: Isn't the principal a dummy! Girl: Do you know who I am? Boy: No. Girl: I'm the principal's daughter. Boy: And do you know who I am? Girl: No. Boy: Thank goodness!

155

Teacher: George, go to the map and find North America. Pupil: Here it is! Teacher: Correct. Now, class, who discovered America? Class: George!

156

Pupil: Teacher, would you punish me for something I didn't do? Teacher: Of course not. Pupil: Good, because I didn't do my homework.

157

Teacher: Why are you late? Pupil: Because of the sign. Teacher: What sign? Pupil: The one that says, "School Ahead, Go Slow."

158

Mother: Why did you get such a low mark on that test? Son: Because of absence. Mother: You mean you were absent on the day of the test? Son: No, but the kid who sits next to me was.

159

Teacher: Ellen, give me a sentence starting with "I". Pupil: I is... Teacher: No, Ellen. Always say, "I am." Pupil: All right... "I am the ninth letter of the alphabet."

160

Mother: Why on earth did you swallow the money I gave you? *Son*: You said it was my lunch money.

161

Teacher: If you received $10 from 10 people, what would you get? *Pupil*: A new bike.

162

Teacher: If I had seven oranges in one hand and eight oranges in the other, what would I have? *Class comedian*: Big hands!

163

Hygiene teacher: How can you prevent diseases caused by biting insects? Pupil: Don't bite any.

164

Teacher: Well, at least there's one thing I can say about your son. *Mother*: What's that? Teacher: With grades like these, he couldn't be cheating.

165

Daughter: Dad, can you write in the dark? *Father*: I think so. What do you want me to write? Daughter: Your name on this report card.

166

A professor was known for being a generous marker. The grades he gave for one of his courses were based solely on two exams and the stuff on the exams was covered entirely in the textbook. As word of the course spread each term there was a large group of students who turned up infrequently, or not at all - just showing up for the exams.

Finally, it got so bad that one term about half of the students never turned up at all until the exams. On the day of first exam, the students sat down and a graduate assistant handed out the papers. The assistant explained: "The professor is ill, so I'll be taking the exams."

When they opened the booklet the students discovered just one question. It listed twenty rather poor quality photos of the academic staff. The instructions read:

"Circle the picture of the professor who teaches this course."

167

Five students were so confident that the weekend before their final exams, they decided to go for a picnic and party with some friends up there. They had a great time. However, after all the partying, they slept all day Sunday and didn't make it back to College until early Monday morning. Rather than taking the final exam then, they decided to find their professor after the final and explain to him why they had missed it. They explained that they had gone to an old people's home in the nearest town to spend some time with aged people for the weekend with the plan to come back and study but, unfortunately, they had a flat tire on the way back, didn't have a spare, and couldn't get help for a long time. As a result, they missed the final exam.

When the Professor had thought it over he agreed they could make up the final the following day. The students were elated and relieved. They studied that night and went in the next day at the time the professor had told them. He placed them in separate rooms and handed each student a test booklet, and told them to begin.

They looked at the first problem, worth 5 points. It was the easiest question in their entire syllabus. "Cool," they thought at the same time, each one in his separate room. "This is going to be easy." Each finished the problem and then turned the page. On the second page was written:

(For 95 points): Which tire?

168

"You will have exactly two hours," said the professor as he handed out examination papers to a roomful of engineering students.

"I will absolutely not accept any papers given to me after the two-hour deadline has passed." Two hours later he broke the silence.

"Time is up," he said. But one student continued to work furiously.

Almost 15 minutes later, the student went up to the professor who was sitting behind the pile of examination papers handed in by the other students.

When the professor refused to accept the student's paper, the student drew himself up to his full height and asked: "Professor, do you know who I am?"

"No," said the professor.

"Terrific," replied the student and stuffed his paper into the middle of the pile of the other examination papers.

169

Johnny has said all the letters from H to O. The chemical formula for water is H2O. *to* and 2 (*two*) sound the same.

170

The chairman of the Board Of Education has mistaken the teacher for one of the boys.

171

'Bright' means 'very light' (like the sun's light), hence the need for dark glasses. But 'bright' also means 'intelligent' and 'smart'.

172

'Cross-eyes' is a medical condition where one or both eyes are turned inwards towards the nose. The 'pupil' is the black part in the middle of your eye, but 'pupil' is also another word for 'student' in a school class.

173

The taxi driver went to the same university as the graduates. The joke is trying to make the point that in times of financial crisis, one doesn't always get the job one studies for.

174

Johnny thinks that the criminal must have been in police custody when the criminal's photo was taken.

175

Johnny wants the rule that applies to him to apply to the teacher too.

Glossary for Chapter 7

astounded	very surprised
bright	intelligent
cheat	copy from another person
coachsports	trainer
dad	daddyfather
deserve	merit
downcast	unhappy
dragged	pulled
elated	happy
fancy	sophisticated
field trip	school trip
free the slaves	liberated the non-free citizens
get	*obtain a result* in math, *buy* when you receive money from a person
grab	take hold of
grade	score
hand it in	consign
handed in	consigned
have back	return
hijacked	taken over by terrorists
jack	the card that comes between a ten and a queen in a pack of cards
kindergarten	school for very young children
make it back	manage to return
mark	score, to assign a score
paper	sheet of paper with answers given by a student in a written test
pile	lots of papers on top of each other
prevent	avoid
principal	head of school
relieved	not anxious any more
report card	card showing a pupil's results in all the subjects. Generally this card has to be shown to the parents who then have to sign it to prove that they have read it
settle down	stop changing

show up	come
solely	only
spare	an extra tire
stuck	put
stuffed	inserted
summon	ask officially to come
swallow	allow food or drink to go down one's throat and into one's stomach
tacked	attached
this once	just for this occasion
tire	rubber that covers the wheel of a car
turn up	attend
unruly	noisy and disorganized
youngster	young person

Chapter 8
Light Bulbs, Waiters, What's the Difference?

Introduction

This chapter consists of three types of standard jokes:

- light bulb
- waiter, waiter
- what's the difference?

Below is a brief explanation of how all these types of joke of work. Some examples and explanations have been drawn from Wikipedia.

LIGHT BULB

The first light bulb jokes were typically used to insult the intelligence of another profession. Below is the archetypal version of the joke, in which we are asked how many people are required to carry out the basic operation of changing (or screwing out and in) a light bulb. Essentially you can insert the name of any profession into the space and make them immediately appear stupid or to fit the stereotype that others have of them.

Q. How many _____ does it take to change a light bulb?
A. Three. One to hold the light bulb and two to turn the ladder.

There are now over 700 versions of this joke (see eyrie.org/~thad/strange/lightbulbs.html for a long list), and several of these versions contain puns on the words "change" and "screw" (which also means 'treat really badly').

Q. How many psychiatrists does it take to change a light bulb?
A. None–the light bulb will change when it's ready.
Q: How many consultants does it take to change a light bulb?
A: We don't know they never get past the feasibility study.

Most of the jokes just consist of a question and a short answer (as in the above examples). But some are incredibly long - more than 500 words.

Match the questions in 176 with the answers.

176

How many consultants does it take to change a light bulb?
How many managers does it take to change a light bulb?
How many shipping department personnel does it take to change a light bulb?
How many senior Presidential aides does it take to change a light bulb?
How many voyeurs does it take to change a light bulb?
How many politicians does it take to change a light bulb?

   a) I'll have an estimate for you a week from Monday.
   b) None. They're supposed to keep the President in the dark.
   c) Only one, but they'd much rather watch someone else do it.
   d) Four, one to change it and the other three to deny it.
   e) We can change the light bulb in seven to ten working days, but if you call before 2 p.m. and pay an extra $15, we can get the bulb changed overnight.
   f) We've formed a task force to study the problem of why light bulbs burn out and to figure out what, exactly, we as supervisors can do to make the bulbs work smarter, not harder.

[shipping - delivery; voyeurs - someone who gets pleasure from watching someone else doing something; keep someone in the dark - hide information from someone; deny - say something isn't true or hasn't been done; task force - special group of experts; figure out - understand]

In some of the cases below (177) the answers match the questions, but not in all cases. Find the answers that don't match and the preceding question, and then relocate them to their correct position.

177

Q: How many economists does it take to screw in a light bulb?
A: 45. One to change the bulb, and 44 to do the paperwork.
Q: How many Republicans does it take to screw in a light bulb?
A: None, they only screw the poor.
Q: How many Russians does it take to change a light bulb?
A: None, it's a waste of time because the new bulb probably won't work either.
Q: How many safety inspectors does it take to change a light bulb?
A: Four. One to change it and three to hold the ladder.
Q: How many civil servants does it take to change the light bulb?
A: None. If the light bulb really needed changing, market forces would have already caused it to happen.
Q: How many archaeologists does it take to change a light bulb?
A: Three. One to change it and two to argue about how old the old one is.
Q: How many pessimists does it take to screw in a light bulb?
A: That's a military secret.

[screw the poor - exploit poor people; ladder - equipment used for climbing up/down something; market forces - factors affecting the price and availability of a product; argue - discuss angrily; pessimist - someone who always sees the negative side]

Fill in the gaps with an appropriate profession from the list below.

- accountants
- Apple programmers
- magicians
- missionaries
- polite native New Yorkers
- psychiatrists
- surrealist painters

178

How many _____ does it take to change a light bulb?

Only one, but the bulb has got to really want to change.

How many _____ does it take to change a light bulb?

What kind of answer did you have in mind?

How many _____ does it take to change a light bulb?

Depends on what you want it to change into.

How many _____ does it take to change a light bulb?

101. One to change it and 100 to convince everyone else to change light bulbs too.

How many _____ does it take to change a light bulb?

Two. One to hold the giraffe, and the other to fill the bathtub with brightly colored machine tools.

How many _____ does it take to change a light bulb?

Both of them.

How many _____ does it take to change a light bulb?

Only one, but why bother? Your light socket will be obsolete in six months.

[polite - with good manners; considerate - thinking about the needs of someone else; surrealist - artist who wishes to release the creative potential of the unconscious mind; have in mind - think of; light socket - hole where the bulb fits; obsolete - out of date and unusable]

Can you understand why the following light bulb joke (179) is funny?

179
A: One.
Q: How many psychics does it take to change a light bulb?

WAITER, WAITER

Waiter, waiter jokes work in a similar way to *doctor, doctor* jokes (see Chapter 2 By beginning the joke with *waiter waiter* the joker informs the listener that the context of the joke is a restaurant.

Here is an example:

> Waiter, there's a fly in my soup.
>
> No sir, that's a spider, the fly is on your steak.

The first line is always said by the customer at the restaurant, who calls over the waiter to ask a question or to make a complaint.

The second line is the response of the waiter.

Below is another example. In this case the joke is connected to the possible ambiguity of the word *serve*, which means in this joke both to *cook* and to *offer services to a client*.

> Waiter, waiter, do you serve fish?
>
> Yes, take a seat madam, we serve anybody.

And here is a variation of the above joke:

> Waiter, waiter, do you serve shrimps?
>
> We serve anyone sir, we don't mind what size you are.

In the first line, the listener is thinking that the customer simply wants to know whether fish is on the menu. The second line, said by the waiter, changes our perspective, and makes fish seem like a type of customer, rather than something to eat.

Waiter, waiter jokes are particularly enjoyed by young children.

Match the beginnings with the endings (a-e) in the jokes in 180.

180

Waiter, there's a dead fly in my soup.
Waiter, there's a fly in my soup.
Waiter, what's this fly doing in my soup?
Waiter, there are two flies in my soup!
Waiter, there is a beetle in my soup!

    a) Don't tell anyone else sir or everyone will be wanting one.
    b) Sorry sir, we're out of flies today!
    c) That's alright sir, have the extra one on me!
    d) Um, looks to me like backstroke, madam.
    e) Yes sir I expect it's the hot water that kills them.

[fly - insect, beetle - insect, backstroke - swimming style]

Insert the verbs below into the correct places for the jokes in 181

    a) crawling
    b) drowning
    c) laughing
    d) learning
    e) talking
    f) trying

181

Waiter, this soup tastes funny! Then why aren't you _____?

Waiter, what's this fly doing in my soup? It looks like it's _____ to swim sir.

Waiter, my lunch is _____ to me! Well you did ask for a tongue sandwich!

Waiter, what is this spider doing in my soup! _____ by the look of it sir!

Waiter, what is this bug _____ on my wife's shoulder! I don't know - friendly thing, isn't he!

Waiter, what is this bug doing in my salad? _____ to find it's way out sir!

[crawling - moving with stomach on the ground; drowning - dying in water; by the look of it - it would seem; bug - insect; find it's way out - escape]

Choose the correct tense for the jokes in 182. Note that slugs, maggots, snails, mosquitoes, creepy-crawlies and flies are all insects or mollusks typically found in a vegetable garden.

182

Waiter, there is a small slug in this lettuce!

    I'm sorry sir, *do/would* you like me to get you a bigger one?

Waiter, there is a slug in my salad!

    I'm sorry sir, I *didn't realize/haven't realized* you where a vegetarian!

Waiter, there is a maggot in my soup!

    Don't worry sir, he *doesn't/won't* last long in there!

Waiter, there's a fly in my soup!

    I fetch/I'll fetch him a spoon sir!

Waiter, are there snails on the menu!

    Yes sir, they *must escape/must have escaped* from the kitchen!

Waiter, there is a mosquito in my soup!

    Don't worry sir, they *don't/won't* eat much!

Waiter, there is a slug in my salad!

    Shhh, or everyone *is wanting/will want* one!

Waiter, what *does this creepy-crawly do/is this creepy-crawly doing* in my salad?

    Not him again, he's in here every night!

Waiter, can you get rid of this fly in my starter!

    I can't do that sir, *he's not had/he did not have* his main course yet!

Waiter, there is a fly in my soup!

    Just you wait until you *see/will see* the main course!

Insert the words and phrases (a-g) below into the correct spaces in the jokes in 183. Note that caterpillars, cockroaches, slugs, spiders and flies are all insects or mollusks typically found in a vegetable garden.

a) don't seem to care
b) ice cream
c) no extra charge
d) no pets allowed
e) plate
f) scared
g) walked

183

Waiter, there's a caterpillar on my salad

Don't worry sir, there is _____ .

Waiter, there is a cockroach on my steak!

They _____ what they eat do they sir?

Waiter, there is a slug in my salad!

Sorry madam, _____ !

Waiter, there is a worm on my _____ !

That's not a worm sir, it's your sausage?

Waiter, there is a spider on my plate, send me the manager!

That's no good, he's _____ of them too!

Waiter, why is there a fly in my _____ ?

Perhaps he likes winter sports!

Waiter, do you have frogs' legs?

No sir, I've always _____ like this.

WHAT'S THE DIFFERENCE?

In a *what's the difference between* joke, two nouns with apparently no connection are juxtaposed.

For example:

> What's the difference between a jeweler and a jailer?
>
> One sells watches, the other watches cells.

In the second line *one* stands for the first noun (i.e. jeweler) and *the other* stands for the second noun (i.e. jailer).

In all cases, the jokes revolve around a play with the sound and meanings of the key words e.g. sells watches vs *watches cells*. In this case *sells* and *cells* have an identical pronunciation but totally different meaning. In the case of *watches*, the first is an instrument for telling the time, the second is a verb meaning to observe.

Note: To understand many of these jokes you need to have a high standard of English.

Your task is simply to try and understand the word play in the following jokes. There is no glossary as the meaning is explained in the key.

184

What's the difference between a cat and a comma?

A cat has claws at the end of its paws, a comma is a pause at the end of a clause.

185

What's the difference between a wet day and a lion with toothache?

One's pouring with rain, the other's roaring with pain.

186

What's the difference between a cashier and a school teacher?

One minds the till, the other tills the mind.

187

What's the difference between a locomotive engineer and a school teacher

One minds the train, the other trains the mind.

188

What's the difference between a fisherman and a lazy schoolboy?

One baits his hook, the other hates his book.

189

What's the difference between a person late for the train, and a teacher in a girls' school?

One misses the train, the other trains the misses.

190

What's the difference between a professional pianist giving a concert, and a member of their audience?

One plays for their pay, the other pays for their play.

191

What's the difference between a glutton and a hungry man?

One eats too long, the other longs to eat.

192

What's the difference between a retired sailor and a blind man?

One cannot go to sea, the other cannot see to go.

193

What's the difference between a lift and the person who runs it?

One is lowered to take passengers up, the other is hired to do it.

194

What's the difference between a hill and a pill?

One is hard to get up, the other is hard to get down.

195

What's the difference between an elephant and a flea?

An elephant can have fleas, but a flea cannot have elephants.

196

What's the difference between a small blue whale and a great white whale?

Size and color.

Read the following 'What's the difference?' jokes - do you think that the butt (i.e. the object of contempt/ridicule) of the joke is men or women?

197

What is the difference between men and government bonds? Bonds mature.

What is the difference between a man and a vulture? A vulture waits until you're dead before ripping your heart out.

What is the difference between a sofa and a man watching football? The sofa doesn't keep asking for beer.

What is the difference between Big Foot and intelligent man? Big Foot's been spotted a several times.

What is the difference between men and women? A woman wants one man to satisfy her every need. A man wants every woman to satisfy his one need.

[government bond - statement issued by government promising to pay borrowed money; vulture - large bird famous for eating dead animals; rip out - remove by force; Big Foot - fictional yeti; spotted - seen by chance;]

Finally, here are three jokes for TEFL teachers taken from teachertalktimes.wordpress.com/tefl-jokes/. Maybe someone would like to email me an explanation of Jokes 199 and 200, because I just don't get them!

198

Teacher: Why did the chicken cross the road?

Student: Sorry, could you repeat?

Teacher: Why did the chicken cross the road?

Student: Because....er.....because....

Other student: We don't know. Why do you always ask us? Why don't you just tell us?

Teacher: Because I'm eliciting! It's what my trainer told me to do!

199

Jimmy was on the first day of his TEFL course. He put up his hand during a seminar, and asked the trainer the following question:

'Excuse me. Why must we do a gist reading before a detailed reading?'

The trainer smiled. 'Because that's what the book says!' As you can imagine, the rest of the group burst into laughter.

200

How many CELTA trainers does it take to change a light bulb?

Two. One to change it, and the other to point and say "You're doing it wrong, now get out of the room."

Key to Chapter 8

176

Q: How many consultants does it take to change a light bulb? A: I'll have an estimate for you a week from Monday.

Q: How many managers does it take to change a light bulb? A: We've formed a task force to study the problem of why light bulbs burn out and to figure out what, exactly, we as supervisors can do to make the bulbs work smarter, not harder.

Q: How many shipping department personnel does it take to change a light bulb? A: We can change the light bulb in seven to ten working days, but if you call before 2 p.m. and pay an extra $15, we can get the bulb changed overnight.

Q: How many senior Presidential aides does it take to change a light bulb? A: None. They're supposed to keep the President in the dark.

Q. How many voyeurs does it take to change a light bulb? A: Only one, but they'd much rather watch someone else do it.

Q: How many politicians does it take to change a light bulb? A: Four, one to change it and the other three to deny it.

177

How many economists does it take to screw in a light bulb? A: None. If the light bulb really needed changing, market forces would have already caused it to happen.

How many Republicans does it take to screw in a light bulb? A: None, they only screw the poor.

How many Russians does it take to change a light bulb? A: That's a military secret.

How many safety inspectors does it take to change a light bulb? A: Four. One to change it and three to hold the ladder.

How many civil servants does it take to change the light bulb? A: 45. One to change the bulb, and 44 to do the paperwork.

How many archaeologists does does it take to change a light bulb? A: Three. One to change it and two to argue about how old the old one is. Q: How many pessimists does it take to screw in a light bulb? A: None, it's a waste of time because the new bulb probably won't work either.

178

How many *psychiatrists* does it take to change a light bulb? Only one, but the bulb has got to really want to change.

How many *accountants* does it take to change a light bulb? What kind of answer did you have in mind?

How many *magicians* does it take to change a light bulb? Depends on what you want it to change into.

How many *missionaries* does it take to change a light bulb? 101. One to change it and 100 to convince everyone else to change light bulbs too.

How many *surrealists* does it take to change a light bulb? Two. One to hold the giraffe, and the other to fill the bathtub with brightly colored machine tools.

How many *New Yorkers etc* does it take to change a light bulb? Both of them.

How many *Apple programmers* does it take to change a light bulb? Only one, but why bother? Your light socket will just be obsolete in six months anyway.

179

Physics predict the answer before you even ask them the question.

180

Waiter, there's a dead fly in my soup. Yes sir I expect it's the hot water that kills them.

Waiter, there's a fly in my soup. Don't tell anyone else sir or everyone will be wanting one.

Waiter, what's this fly doing in my soup? Um, looks to me like backstroke, madam.

Waiter, there are two flies in my soup! That's alright sir, have the extra one on me!

Waiter, there is a beetle in my soup! Sorry sir, we're out of flies today!

181

Waiter, this soup tastes funny! Then why aren't you laughing?

Waiter, what's this fly doing in my soup? It looks like it's learning to swim sir.

Waiter, my lunch is talking to me! Well you did ask for a tongue sandwich!

Waiter, what is this spider doing in my soup! Drowning by the look of it sir!

Waiter, what is this bug crawling on my wife's shoulder! I don't know - friendly thing isn't he!

Waiter, what is bug doing in my salad?

Trying to find it's way out sir!

182

Waiter, there is a small slug in this lettuce! I'm sorry sir, *would* you like me to get you a bigger one?

Waiter, there is a slug in my salad! I'm sorry sir, I *didn't realize* you where a vegetarian!

Waiter, there is a maggot in my soup! Don't worry sir, he *won't* last long in there!

Waiter, there's a fly in my soup! *I'll fetch* him a spoon sir!

Waiter, are there snails on the menu! Yes sir, they *must have escaped* from the kitchen!

Waiter, there is a mosquito in my soup! Don't worry sir, they *don't* eat much!

Waiter, there is a slug in my salad! Shhh, or everyone *will want* one!

Waiter, what *is this creepy-crawly doing* in my salad? Not him again, he's in here every night!

Waiter, can you get rid of this fly in my starter! I can't do that sir, *he's not had* his main course yet!

Waiter, there is a fly in my soup! Just you wait until you *see* the main course!

183

Waiter, there's a caterpillar on my salad. Don't worry sir, there is *no extra charge*.

Waiter, there is a cockroach on my steak! They *don't seem to care* what they eat do they sir?

Waiter, there is a slug in my salad! Sorry madam, *no pets allowed*!

Waiter, there is a worm on my *plate*! That's not a worm sir, it's your sausage?

Waiter, there is a spider on my plate, send me the manager! That's no good, he's *scared* of them too!

Waiter, why is there a fly in my *ice cream*? Perhaps he likes winter sports!

Waiter, do you have frogs legs? No sir, I've always *walked* like this.

184

claws - the animal equivalent of human nails, *paws* - the animal equivalent of human feet

a comma indicates a *pause* at the end of a *clause* (phrase)

185

to pour with rain is what happens on a wet day (i.e. it rains very hard)

to roar - the very load noise lions make

186

minds the till - to look after the cash box

tills the mind - stimulates the brain

187

minds the train - is responsible for the correct running of the train

trains the mind - educates the brain

188

bait is what a fisherman uses to attract fish, the hook is what goes into the fish's mouth to enable the fisherman to catch it

189

trains the misses - educates the girls (miss = unmarried woman)

Key to Chapter 8

190

a musician plays in order to earn money

the audience pays in order to hear the musicians play

191

eats too long - eats for a very long time

longs to eat - has a strong desire to eat

192

If a sailor is retired he no longer goes on a ship on the sea.

A blind man cannot see where is he going.

193

lowered - goes down (and up)

hired sounds like *highered* (i.e. the opposite of *lowered*); *hired* means employed

194

a pill (medication) is hard to get down your throat in the sense that you need water to enable you to swallow it

195

when an animal has fleas it has parasites living on its skin. But obviously a flea does not have an elephant living on its skin!

196

This is a joke about 'what's the difference' jokes. It answers in a literal way.

197

The butt is men in every case.

198

To *elicit* - a means to enable the teacher to get information from his/her students rather than simply giving the students the information

199

Reading for *gist*, means reading a text just to get a general idea rather than focusing on the details. However, the meaning of this joke is lost on me!

200

CELTA is an exam for teachers. Again, I don't understand the meaning of the joke. Ask your teacher if he/she can understand it!!

Glossary for Chapter 8

argue	discuss angrily
backstroke	swimming style
beetle	insect
Big Foot	fictional yeti
bug	insect
by the look of it	it would seem
considerate	thinking about the needs of someone else
crawling	moving with stomach on the ground
deny	say something isn't true or hasn't been done
drown	die in water
figure out	understand
find one's way out	escape
fly	insect,
government bond	statement issued by government promising to pay borrowed money
have in mind	think of
keep someone in the dark	hide information from someone
ladder	equipment used for climbing up/down something
light socket	hole where the bulb fits
market forces	factors affecting the price and availability of a product
obsolete	out of date and unusable
pessimist	someone who always sees the negative side
polite	with good manners
rip out	remove by force
screw the poor	exploit poor people
shipping	delivery
spot	see by chance
surrealist	artist who wishes to release the creative potential of the unconscious mind
task force	special group of experts
voyeurs	someone who gets pleasure from watching someone else doing something
vulture	large bird famous for eating dead animals

Index

A
Animals, 1–15
Army, 111

B
Barber's, 63
Bats, 9
Boss, 53
Butcher, 6

C
Cat, 10
Chemist (researcher), 106
Computer, 111
Computer programmer, 105, 107

D
Desert island, 140
Doctors, 19–48, 130, 131
Dog, 1, 6–8
Dracula, 9
Drunks, 50–52, 54, 55

E
Engineer, 105, 107, 113

F
Factory, 53
Fishing, 57
Food, 16–18

G
General Motors, 133
Giraffe, 2
Goldfish, 13
Gorilla, 8, 12

H
Hunters, 11
Husband and wife, 58–63, 128, 132, 140–142

I
Idiots, 49–56

J
Johnny, 143–175

K
Kids at school, 143–175
Knock knock, 64–104

L
Lawyers, 116–124
Light bulb jokes, 176–179

M
Manager, 105
MBA graduates, 114, 115
Men *vs.* women, 58–63, 128, 132, 140–142
Microsoft, 133

O
Old people, 125–127, 129

P
Parrot, 4
Physicist, 106, 107
Pilot, 112
Pit bull, 8
Polar bear, 3
Pub, 12, 15

R
Restaurant, 16–18

S
School, 143–175
School kids, 143–175
Senile, 57, 125–127

Shotgun, 8
Statistician, 106
Student, 110, 114
Students drunk, 50, 51

T
Teachers, 143–175, 198–200
TEFL, 198–200
Tiger, 5
Train, 134
Travel, 134–140

W
Waiter, 180–183
What's the difference, 184–197
Wife and husband, 58–63, 128, 132, 140–142
Women *vs.* men, 58–63, 128, 132, 140–142
Worms, 14

GPSR Compliance

The European Union's (EU) General Product Safety Regulation (GPSR) is a set of rules that requires consumer products to be safe and our obligations to ensure this.

If you have any concerns about our products, you can contact us on

ProductSafety@springernature.com

In case Publisher is established outside the EU, the EU authorized representative is:

Springer Nature Customer Service Center GmbH
Europaplatz 3
69115 Heidelberg, Germany

www.ingramcontent.com/pod-product-compliance
Lightning Source LLC
LaVergne TN
LVHW010342260326
834688LV00036B/842